A Passion for Truth

Comments on the Book

A Jesuit spiritual director: "Each chapter is a unique gift. The dazzle of what you know and how you have used your thirst for truth and goodness, the extraordinary manner of your vocation, your love and admiration for the people in your life, the importance of your work, your radical obedience even in the face of horrid injustice: all this and so much more is the abundant gift you give us in this book… Already an image is forming: Moses inspired by his encounter with the burning bush, Mozart and Beethoven inspired by harmony, and you inspired by the truth of mathematics, chemistry, and orthodoxy."

A university professor: "I sat down yesterday and picked up your manuscript. Darkness descended but in the light of your words I hadn't noticed as I was totally captivated. Thank you for sharing this intimate spiritual biography that has taken so much of your thought over so many years. It provoked great gratitude for how you have been so important in so many ways in my own spiritual journey and for your friendship. It continues to echo in my consciousness."

A Catholic layman: "I did want to say how much I enjoyed your manuscript. I am fascinated about your intellectual bridging of faith and science or reason from the standpoint of your particular expertise in quantum physics. For example, Dr. Frances Collins wrote from the human genome perspective on this, Einstein pursued a unifying theory, and Fr. Robert Barron is explaining the universe from a philosophical viewpoint, but you've got a unique perspective as well."

A Benedictine monk: "John, this book is your apostolate."

A Catholic bishop: "It is gentle but forthright."

A professor of classics: "It is lucidly written."

A senior Dominican priest: "It is concise, but I would add, far ranging."

A layman: "The chapter on Scientific Truth is the most important chapter."

A Passion for Truth

Reflections of a Scientist-Priest

John Huntington

PAGE PUBLISHING, INC.
New York, NY

First originally published by Page Publishing, Inc. 2018

Cover: Baptism of Ruby Catherine Hobbs

ISBN 978-1-64350-078-2 (Paperback)
ISBN 978-1-64350-079-9 (Digital)

Printed in the United States of America

For Judy

Who is the love of my life

Contents

Preface

This book is the product of many years of preparation. It is meant to help its readers to reflect on the world we live in and our place in it. I do not to want convince anyone of anything, but only to open up new ways of thinking. I present my own learning as a personal narrative in order to engage and sustain the interest of readers. This was not an easy decision. We scientists have not been trained to write in the first person and to spill our guts, but rather to write dryly with many footnotes, hardly mentioning ourselves at all.

Over time I have uncovered a number of fallacies embedded in our Western culture that cramp our thinking and hurt us. Those fallacies are sometimes used to advance one or another petty agenda. Exposing them is a principal purpose of this book. A new understanding can be therapeutic, since to name a thing accurately is to gain some control over its effects. At the root of all of those fallacies is the idea that it is acceptable to be careless with the truth. In liberal academic circles this mindset is dignified as "postmodernism," as if it were a new and superior kind of enlightenment; its equivalent in theology it is called "relativism." Uncritically crediting scientists with insights and authority that they do not possess is given the name "scientism." A passion for truth can lift us up above the petty agendas supported by those fallacies to the place where love, justice, freedom and authenticity are to be found. I hope that you will read this book with a supple mind conformable to the truth as you encounter it.

I am a priest to the soles of my feet. I am also a physical scientist to the soles of my feet. My worldview is rooted in objective truth teased out of information received by our natural senses, augmented with observations made by the instruments of physical science. While what we see of the world can be confirmed by consensus, care must always be taken that the outlier who sees something else be heard with patience. Common sense is fallible, and we must be very careful. The observations of physical science are of a different order. You could shoot a physical scientist and break his equipment, but his observations would stand. We would be confident that, were another scientist to come along with the interest and resources to do so, he could build similar equipment, and he would see the same things. This order of objectivity does not depend on common sense. It is what has given physical science its high reputation, and it is the firm ground on which my worldview stands.

The language of physical science is mathematics. If, as I argue, quantum mechanics is the physics of fundamental processes, we have a problem: we cannot easily talk about it. Even today, about ninety years since the discovery of quantum mechanics, the principles of quantum mechanics are not widely understood by our people. But all is not lost. There are two ways that one could say a person understands quantum mechanics. One could spend years in graduate school acquiring an MS in Mathematics and the set of mathematical rules that constitute the subject in order to be competent to define, formulate and solve practical problems using quantum mechanics, or one could simply study the phenomena that are characteristic of quantum mechanics and that can be described in ordinary language, as I have done here. For the sake of the narrative flow, I will use terms freely that I do not stop to explain. Though I expect that you will find the Bibliography helpful, I trust that you will use the internet to delve further. The resources available on the internet far exceed the wonders of the library in ancient Alexandria. Whether your question be one of physical science or theology and I do not stop to explain, please just Google it.

The Catechism of the Catholic Church, a book of 904 pages, is only the second comprehensive catechism published by the Vatican in two thousand years. It was commissioned and promulgated by Pope John Paul II to provide a systematic presentation of the Catholic Christian faith. It is a product of the *Magisterium*, that is, the teaching authority of the Church. It says the following regarding truth: "Truth as uprightness in human action and speech is called *truthfulness*, sincerity, or candor. Truth or truthfulness is the virtue which consists in showing oneself true in deeds and truthful in words, and in guarding against duplicity, dissimulation, and hypocrisy."… "Thus, the pastoral duty of the *Magisterium* is aimed at seeing to it that the People of God abides in the truth that liberates" and further, "Man tends by nature toward the truth. He is obliged to honor and bear witness to it: 'It is in accordance with their dignity that all men, because they are persons…are both impelled by their nature and bound by a moral obligation to seek the truth, especially religious truth. They are also bound to adhere to the truth once they come to know it and direct their whole lives in accordance with the demands of truth.'" Relativism in its religious sense is an attack on the unique truth claims of Catholic Christianity, that is, of dogmatic theology. It cannot be accepted as the basis for ecumenical or interfaith dialogue.

On Bullshit, a beautiful little essay by Princeton professor emeritus of philosophy Harry Frankfurt, explores the troubling cultural phenomenon of being careless with the truth. It seems acceptable to say anything one wants to on any subject, without consequences. Everything must be permitted, and nothing seems to matter. I thank God for the corrective tonic of Professor Frankfurt's clear thinking.

The glossary of the Public Broadcasting System website www.pbs.org offers the following definition of postmodernism: "A general and wide-ranging term which is applied to literature, art, philosophy, architecture, fiction, and cultural literary criticism, among others. Postmodernism is largely a reaction to the assumed certainty of scientific, or objective, efforts to explain reality. In essence, it stems from a recognition that reality is not simply mirrored in human understanding of it, but rather, is constructed as the mind tries to understand its own particular and personal reality. For this reason, postmodernism is highly skeptical of explanations which claim to be valid for all groups, cultures, traditions, or races, and instead focuses on the relative truths of each person."

Carelessness in physical science is a stone on my heart. I see it almost everywhere. As a community, we physical scientists know how to do things right. Too few of us bother to do so. We could begin by writing and speaking in the subjunctive mood when addressing hypothetical ideas. Why not be clear about what is a hypothesis and what is a law? Why not be clear about the limitations of physical science? Why not be examples of trustworthiness?

In *The Passion of the Western Mind* Richard Tarnas describes the ancient Sophists as, in effect, the postmodernists of their day. To counter their influence, Socrates rose up, "a man of singular character and intelligence, who was imbued with a passion for intellectual honesty and moral integrity rare for his or any other age... His words and deeds embodied an abiding conviction that the act of rational self-criticism could free the human mind from the bondage of false opinion... Disarmingly humble yet presumptuously confident, puckishly witty yet morally urgent, engaging and gregarious yet solitary and contemplative, Socrates was a man consumed by a passion for truth."

Our intellect and will are gifts from God that mark us as human. To be faithful to our Creator we must strive for clarity of mind as an act of loving obedience. May God bless your inquiry.

How to Read this Book

Make a glossary, using a word processor. Share it with a discussion group. This could be a college seminar class or a book club. Update the glossary as your understanding deepens. Work toward definitions that ring most true. With e-mail and Skype, members of a discussion group could be anywhere. Give one another the courage to challenge conventional wisdom. Bravo!

Acknowledgments

I gratefully acknowledge the nurture I received from
my aunt Gladys and uncle Hermann Burian,
who welcomed me into their home
at the University of Iowa;
my scientific fathers
Joseph Hirschfelder and John Ross;
and
my spiritual fathers
Canon Douglas Williams; Thomas Schultz, OHC; Bernard
Bush, SJ; Vincent Hovley, SJ; and Carleton Jones, OP.

I am most grateful for the hospitality extended to me
by the Society of Jesus at
El Retiro Jesuit Retreat House of Los Altos, California;
Santa Clara University;
Sacred Heart Jesuit Retreat House in Sedalia, Colorado;
and Woodstock (Jesuit) Theological Center at Georgetown
University, where it was my privilege to serve as a
Senior Fellow.

This book was written in fulfillment of promises made to
Prof. André Delbecq and Vincent Hovley, SJ.

Some of the ideas in this book were first aired
in the Colorado Catholic Herald.

Charlie

In the spring of 1945 in the dusty little town of Socorro, New Mexico, our family experienced a tragedy that changed my life. My little brother Charlie drowned, and I became a philosopher. It happened this way.

Dad heard that big catfish were being caught in the irrigation ditches along the Rio Grande, and we were off. We met Ash Henderson at a bridge over a pair of ditches that carried torrents of brown water. Ash was an engineer who worked for Dad at the manganese mine outside of town. Dad and Ash rigged their rods and got to fishing in the water just downstream of the bridge. My older brother Richard and I rigged up as quickly as we could. Men and boys were fishing for big catfish. But Charlie was with us. Our pickup was parked on the bridge with its doors wide open, a bag of potato chips on the seat. A gust of wind blew the chips out the door and onto the road on the upstream side, where Charlie bent down to get them. That was the last time I saw him. He was found in the water eight days later. He had been trapped against an iron grating right where he fell. Dickie Lehmann told me that he saw Charlie on the examining table in his father's office. He said that Charlie was all swollen and black. He was two years old.

Dad and Ash called for Charlie and looked everywhere for him, but he did not answer. At last Dad told Ash to stay, that he would take us home and get the sheriff to get a search going. I knew that he would have to tell Mother. This was awful. On the way to town I asked, "Dad, will they put you in jail?" "No." Then silence. I was there when he told Mother that Charlie was missing. Disbelief and grief possessed us all.

A search was organized by the sheriff. Footprints were found in the desert that were compared to Charlie's shoes. Sightings and bits of clothing were reported. Then one day at school a Carmelite sister said, "They found your brother." We ran home. She had not told us that he was dead.

I could not believe that Charlie's life was ended. I could not stand to hear the word "death." I forgot how to smile. Sometimes marriages fail after the death of a child. That is what happened to our family.

Newly divorced, Mother arrived in New York in August 1948 with a four-month-old son, Jimmy, and no job. Richard and I remained behind in New Mexico with Dad until she was settled and could call for us. She was resolved to work for the United Nations. She spoke seven languages, five of them fluently, and she very much believed in the mission of the UN. She had earned a PhD from a prestigious German university. Her problem was that she was a now a naturalized US citizen, and there was a quota. The UN is an international organization, and the management was intent that the mix of its employees reflect its membership. We had to survive on her temporary appointments until, after several years, she finally received a permanent position. During that time Dad provided little financial support. Friends, aware of our need, once dropped a basket of food on our doorstep. Mother managed to find a series of immigrant women to live with us for room and board and a little money. Their responsibility was to take care of Jimmy during the week, and to be there when we got home from school. Things were very thin, but not at Christmas. Somehow, Mother always managed to make Christmas wonderful for us boys. She knew just what things we most wanted to add to our American Flyer electric train set. We always had a Christmas tree done up in good German style, with tinsel like liquid silver hung stand by strand, and lighted with real candles to make it all shimmer. Each of us could count on music and a book. She chose music and reading for us that honored our intelligence and formed our tastes. She joined a pool at the UN that brought her occasional tickets to the New York Philharmonic. I never missed a chance to go with her. She was always looking out for opportunities for our enrichment. And she knew me. She always knew who I am. Of that I was certain. Her regard for me gave me all the strength that I would need later in life.

I became very quiet in New York. It was an interesting life among the eight million people in that great city. They seemed not to know how to behave. This was not Socorro, where people looked you in the eye and said, "Good morning." I withdrew into a richly varied interior life of books. I read everything, and began developing philosophically. I thought about becoming an astronomer. I learned the properties of the great telescopes. I had a star map over my bed. And I had a great project. It became intensely important to me to become a good person. By this I meant that I would in time learn how to avoid hurting people. When I imagined that I had hurt someone by something I said or did, I suffered intense pangs of remorse and resolved to do better. This occupied much of my time and thought. I missed Dad fiercely. My depression lasted eight years from the time of Charlie's death.

Charles Morgan Huntington was born on March 13, 1943 in Silver City, New Mexico. He died on April 26, 1945 in an irrigation ditch outside of Socorro, New Mexico. His body was recovered on May 4. He is buried in Albuquerque.

Maria Luise Burian was born in Leipzig, Germany August 4, 1908. She was married to Morgan Huntington for eleven years and bore him four sons. She obtained the PhD in art history at the University of Leipzig. After divorcing Morgan, she began a career in the United Nations. She died of Alzheimer's, in our home. She is buried with her father in Iowa City, Iowa.

The University of Wisconsin

As a student in high school and university I slowly became fascinated with the idea of applying the methods of mathematical physics to problems in chemistry. I cannot say just why this happened but I can say how it happened. In my junior year in high school I had an excellent physics teacher named Harvey Pollack. His teaching was so good and so clear that I never needed to open the textbook. I received 100% on all of the examinations and an A grade on all the extra credit problems. He noticed me. One morning as I was walking to school he drove by and stopped. He offered me a ride to school and took advantage of the few minutes we had to pose a problem. He asked me how the pilot of an airplane could know where he was if he were flying in the clouds. Using radar to see ground objects was not permitted. Nor was dead reckoning. He was apparently trying to get me to invent inertial navigation in less than 15 minutes. I am afraid that I disappointed him. But I considered the question he asked me to be a compliment. He thought I had a gift for physics, and I noticed. I have treasured his good opinion for the rest of my life.

The clarity of my physics class was not matched by my experience in chemistry. Right off the bat I found a lack of clarity. It seemed to be more of an art than a science. How does one define "valence?" How is it measured? I could get no satisfaction from our teacher or our textbook. I took a long bus ride to a city library with its many reference books and spent the afternoon looking for a satisfactory definition. I found no joy there.

Later, in my junior year in university as a chemistry major I found physics, mathematics and chemistry intimately joined in the subject of physical chemistry. I concluded that the best way forward toward a PhD would be in that subject. I was convinced that, **to the degree that the methods of mathematical physics were successfully applied to any subject, that subject would become more truly a *physical* science, and more objective, and more secure**. This line of study in graduate school would make good use of my love of physics and mathematics, and it would build on my study of chemistry. That was my logic, and that was what brought me to the University of Wisconsin one sparkling autumn day. I was aware that the University of Wisconsin had an outstanding group of professors of physical chemistry. But I was not ready for the surprise I received that day. I did not know about Joe Hirschfelder. I did not know that he had received dual PhDs from Princeton University in physics and chemistry. I did not know that his PhD advisors were both Nobel laureates. I did not know that he had been the youngest scientist in the Manhattan Project. Filled with enthusiasm about my idea, I barged into the Chemistry Department and started explaining myself to a very surprised receptionist. I told her that I wanted to come to Wisconsin to study physical chemistry because of my enthusiasm for applying the methods of mathematical physics to problems in chemistry. She said, "You should talk with Professor Cornwell." I knew his name because he was co-author of a laboratory book I had used in my physical chemistry study at the University of Iowa. I went down the hall to his office and stood in his doorway and began my recitation. He was a young man with a crew cut and a bow tie, well turned out and alert. He quickly said, "You should talk with

Professor Hirschfelder." He called ahead, and I went to the corner of the campus where I found the low, cinderblock building that was the Naval Research Laboratory. Joe Hirschfelder had a large, spare office there. I found him at his desk and began my recitation.

This time it was no monologue. I was expressing my own excitement for what was, after all, his life's work. Anyone who had the good fortune to know this man will tell you about his enthusiasm for his work, and how everything he did was "fun." We both waved our arms and showed our enthusiasm in a kind of duet. This was a most remarkable interview. He accepted me into his graduate program, and I showed up in June of 1962. The Naval Research Laboratory was about to become the Theoretical Chemistry Institute, directed by Prof. Hirschfelder himself. In an interview with the *Wisconsin State Journal* the week I arrived he said, "The setup will be unique, and will give us an opportunity to lead developments about to break in this field. We will be especially helped by the excellent theoretical physics and applied mathematics groups at the University." I was in on the ground floor, and I was in heaven.

What is theoretical chemistry? A review article by Linus Pauling in 1928 defined the subject. Let us take a brief look at the history recounted in his paper, *The Application of the Quantum Mechanics to the Structure of the Hydrogen Molecule and Hydrogen Molecule-Ion and to Related Problems* published on July 1 of that year. The language in that paper seems quaint to me today, but we must remember how new "the quantum mechanics" was at the time. It was only three years since Werner Heisenberg's foundational publication, and two years since Erwin Schroedinger's independent formulation of quantum mechanics. Many theoreticians got busy finding out whether this new quantum mechanics worked. The "old quantum mechanics" of Neils Bohr did not. Would the new theory explain why two hydrogen atoms could form a diatomic molecule and why two helium atoms could not? Would it match up with spectroscopic data on the electronic energy levels of those simple molecules and ions? Pauling's paper concluded that the new version of quantum mechanics had triumphed. Thus was the discipline of theoretical chemistry born. He wrote, "The straightforward application of the quantum mechanics results in the unambiguous conclusion that two hydrogen atoms will form a molecule but that two helium atoms will not; for this distinction is characteristically chemical, and its clarification marks the genesis of sub-atomic theoretical chemistry." Today we can say that **quantum mechanics explains the chemical bond, and therefore in principle, all of chemistry.** Chemistry was on the way to becoming a truly physical science.

Joe Hirschfelder taught us quantum mechanics from the 1935 textbook *An Introduction to Quantum Mechanics with Applications to Chemistry* by Linus Pauling and E. Bright Wilson. It employed the formulation of Erwin Schroedinger, which is most appropriate for systems in stationary states, that is, states that are stable for long times if left undisturbed. Let me tell you about that book. It is a monument to the energy and insight of its authors. I love the book so much that I want to tell you all about it. But let me just give you its Table of Contents:

I.   Survey of Classical Mechanics

II.   The Old Quantum Theory

III. The Schroedinger Wave Equation with the Harmonic Oscillator as an Example

IV. The Wave Equation for a System of Point Particles in Three Dimensions

V. The Hydrogen Atom

VI. Perturbation Theory

VII. The Variation Method and Other Approximate Methods

VIII. The Spinning Electron and the Pauli Exclusion Principle, with a Discussion of the Helium Atom

IX. Many-Electron Atoms

X. The Rotation and Vibration of Molecules

XI. Perturbation Theory Involving the Time, the Emission and Absorption of Radiation, and the Resonance Phenomenon

XII. The Structure of Simple Molecules

XIII. The Structure of Complex Molecules

XIV. Miscellaneous Applications of Quantum Mechanics

XV. General Theory of Quantum Mechanics

This last chapter refers to the "transformation theory" of Paul Dirac, about which more later. The appendixes are full of gems, among which is the information, useful at any cocktail party, that there are exactly eleven orthogonal coordinate systems in three dimensions. Remember, this book was published in 1935, when there were no digital computers. The idea that symbolic mathematics could be done on digital computers, as with Steven Wolfram's *Mathematica,* was far over the horizon. Progress could be made in computational physics only by use of pen on paper, solving problems laboriously, with whatever trick mathematical methods one had in one's toolkit. In this regard, Prof. Hirschfelder posed a question to our class: "How was it possible for Coolidge and James to solve Schroedinger's equation for the ground state energy of the hydrogen molecule-ion electron over two years of effort without making any mistake whatsoever?" Of course, I knew that this would be impossible. Then Joe Hirschfelder showed us how it was done. Soon enough, I needed to use the technique myself.

Hirschfelder had come up with his first-order perturbation iteration method in the hope that it would converge quickly and speed up the kind of approximate, yet accurate, calculations we often found ourselves doing. He now wanted to test the method on simple systems for which the exact solutions were known. He gave me an assignment: apply the method to the perturbed linear harmonic oscillator and compare the asymptotic expansion of the energy expectation value with the eighth order term in the known exact expansion. (I apologize for the language!) This involved integrating Schroedinger's equation iteratively. I completed the task in four months, free of any mistakes. I chose to work with a ballpoint pen on large sheets of art paper, lining out any mistakes and correcting them so that there would be a record of everything I did. At first I could do this only two hours in the morning before I generated too many mistakes to go on. Gradually I got my productive time up to five hours a day, and there it stayed. I would visit Hirschfelder in his office weekly to go over my progress, until we hit a bump in the road. A term had appeared in my calculations that was intractable. It was like a lump of coal in a bowl of rice pudding. It just did not belong. But, there it was. We wrestled with it for a couple of weeks, until one afternoon, as I was riding home on my bicycle, Hirschfelder drove up behind me in his big sedan. There was some distinguished visitor in the passenger seat. Hirschfelder wanted to say something to me. He had an idea for dealing with our problem. He forced my bicycle off the road until I was completely covered by a large bush. He rolled down the passenger's window and shouted his suggestion to me across his amazed guest. From inside the bush I answered, "It vanishes."

"What?"

"It vanishes. The coefficient is zero."

"Are you sure?"

"Yes."

"Good."

He drove off and left me to extract myself from the bush and pedal home.

My work and some companion work by a postdoctoral fellow were written up in an internal report of the Institute and submitted to the Journal of Chemical Physics for publication. In those days there was no desktop publishing, and files of text and mathematical expressions were typed or handwritten on papers submitted to journals. In time one would receive galley proofs from the publisher. These were typeset on glossy paper, and looked quite elegant. Hirschfelder handed me the proof of our paper and a copy of the internal report. Would I please proofread the galley? Would

I mark corrections in red pencil for typos originating with us and in black pencil for those typos made by the publisher? I returned the galley two days later. It was full of penciled corrections, about equally red and black. I recall the shock on his face when I handed it to him. He had not expected this. He had so much emphasized care to his students and staff. I once showed him a correction I had made in the table of coefficients of the Hermite polynomials in the *Handbook of Mathematical Functions* recently published by the National Bureau of Standards. He said, "This is important!" He required me to write to the authors at the NBS with the erratum. In return I received from them a List of Errata for the first edition of the *Handbook*, which Hirschfelder had copied for distribution to the staff and students of the Institute. He was adamant that his students and staff be careful. In those days we depended on handbooks for mathematical resources. None was more ubiquitous than Dwight's *Tables of Integrals and Other Mathematical Data*, until the NBS *Handbook* came out. We became expert at using them. We were students of mathematical tricks.

I must tell you that I was still very shy in graduate school, and very proper. I simply could not call Professor Hirschfelder "Joe," though he encouraged everyone to do so. I always called him "Professor." From early on in my young life I tended to sit by as an observer, getting everything right, but staying on the sidelines. This has been called the "second son syndrome." I was, in fact, a second son. My purpose in graduate school was to become the world's best problem solver. I wanted to become super-competent. I wanted to know what works. I wanted to be always right. I wanted to know how the physical world works, and to be correct in analyzing any physical situation. And, though I did not realize it until much later, I wanted to be helpful. Hirschfelder really liked me and was puzzled by my quietness. He thought I might need psychological help, though I declined. As odd as it might seem, I decided not to take the degree Master of Science in Mathematics because of Hirschfelder's concern for me. It went like this.

During the summer of 1964 Hirschfelder was in residence at a Florida university while I remained in Wisconsin. Since I was taking so many mathematics courses, it occurred to me to inquire about getting an MS in Mathematics. It turned out to be a slam-dunk. I would only need to take one course in the "complex variable" and then pass a one-day examination, and I would be granted the degree. I was using the complex variable in my daily work, and I really did not need that one course, but I would take it to qualify for the degree. I would need to be sponsored by a professor of mathematics. Professor Korevaar kindly agreed to sponsor me, so I was in. Of course, I planned to continue toward the PhD in Chemistry at the Theoretical Chemistry Institute. I wrote about my plan to Hirschfelder in Florida, who quite misunderstood. He thought that I intended to leave physical science for mathematics. That I intended to leave him for Prof. Korevaar. He wrote back a passionate letter that this would be a mistake. That I was to be a scientist, not a mathematician. That I must not do this. I dropped the idea, and never mentioned it again.

Let me add words of gratitude for a stunning young professor of physics at Wisconsin named Adam Bincer. He taught the capstone graduate course in quantum mechanics, which I had the privilege to take. He called his two-semester course "Linear Operator Mechanics," emphasizing the elegant mathematical structure of quantum mechanics. He followed Dirac's transformation theory, which enabled the formulation of problems in a most simple and direct way, so that we could seemingly descend from the clouds to obtain concrete results. I do not know how else to put it. The course was stunningly beautiful, and made me feel certain that I was doing the right thing with my young life. I had the following e-mail exchange with Prof. Bincer in 2008:

Dear Prof. Bincer,

I took your course in Linear Operator Mechanics in the early 1960s and found the experience transformative. I was at the time a student of Joe Hirschfelder in the Theoretical Chemistry Institute. I took the MS at Wisconsin and went on to study with John Ross at Brown and MIT. Brown PhD, 1968. I applied quantum mechanical scattering theory (Tobocman) to reactive molecular beam collisions. It was your course that convinced me that I was doing the right thing with my young life. I found the subject, as presented by you, very beautiful and very compelling. It has been said that all learning is transformative, and that surely was my experience with your course.

I am currently writing a book that is a memoir of ideas, and I would like to correctly refer to my experience with your teaching. Would you kindly forward to me a brief CV for use in my end notes? I would be most grateful.

Thank you.

John H. Huntington

11 February 2008

Professor Bincer replied:

Dear John,

Thank you for your kind words – I find it very rewarding to hear from somebody like you that my teaching made a difference.

Here are some facts of my CV. I was born in 1930 in Krakow, Poland. In 1940 I was deported with my family into the Soviet Union where I spent the Second World War in the Ural Mountains and in Kazakhstan – it is ironic but I owe surviving the war to that deportation.

In 1946 I returned to Poland and shortly afterwards left to go to Sao Paolo, Brazil. I spent two years there repairing radios for a living and came to the US in 1949 to become a freshman at MIT. I planned to study Electrical Engineering to continue to make a living in Brazil. But my real interests were in Mathematics so as a compromise I switched to Physics receiving a BS in 1953 and PhD in 1956 at MIT.

I did some postgraduate research at Brookhaven National Laboratory and then at University of California in Berkeley before coming to Wisconsin as an Assistant Professor in 1960. Most of my research publications are on topics in group theory, sometimes in application to Particle Physics.

I retired in 1996 and now spend my winters in Florida. I would be interested in seeing your book when it is finished – good luck with that.

All the best,

Adam Bincer

12 February 2008

I offer an anecdote from my time in Prof. Bincer's class. During the second semester our class was given a take-home examination on a Friday morning. It was due in class the next Wednesday. I took the exam to my office and addressed the first problem. I stared at it for five hours. After a night's sleep I returned to my office and stared at the problem for another five hours. Then, suddenly, I understood the question and proceeded to solve it quickly and move on to the next. I paused first to ask myself whether the question was a fair one, and well posed. I concluded that it was. It was suitable for a capstone course in quantum mechanics to be taken by PhD candidates in physics. This is the kind of severe testing that must be done in a department of high reputation. I felt privileged to be tested that way. I must tell you that in my office complex there was a graduate student from Korea who could not crack the problem. He repeatedly asked for my help, but I declined to give it. He had run into my hard-nosed attitude about learning: that it is a lonely enterprise. I do think that I was one of Prof. Bincer's better students, even though I sat quietly in the back of the classroom. I am most grateful to have had that brilliant man for my teacher.

The intellectual opportunities for me at the University of Wisconsin were ideal. I could take any course I wanted in physics and mathematics to gain competence for my work in quantum chemistry. The downside to this was the dreaded "cumulative examinations" given by the Chemistry Department. Graduate students wanting to go on for the PhD in chemistry needed to pass five of the twelve exams taken in the second and third years of graduate study. As you might imagine, the exams were designed to be quite challenging. Only half of the students taking an exam would be allowed to pass. This was to separate the sheep from the goats. I turned out to be a goat. I had passed three of the six exams given in my second year and it seemed very likely that I could pass two of the six offered in my third year. But that did not happen. One exam after another was on a graduate chemistry subject I had not taken. Most offerings just did not interest me, and I did not have time for them. We were not told in advance what subject would be covered, so I tried to read the textbooks of all the courses I had not taken. It did not work. A professor knows who has attended his course, who showed interest, and who seemed to "get it." But he would not likely know me. This was like the Chinese water torture. It slowly became clear that I would not make it. The stress of this resulted in a chronic headache from scalp tension and the feeling of a fishbone stuck in my throat. So Hirschfelder swung into action. I think that he felt some responsibility for the mismatch between my coursework and the subjects of the cumulative exams. But he thought I was worth saving. He called me into his office and told me that I would be granted an MS in Chemistry from Wisconsin. He had spoken with Prof. John Ross at Brown University, who had agreed to accept me as a PhD candidate. Was I interested in going to Brown to study with John Ross? Of course, I jumped at the opportunity.

During the summer of 1965 I worked as a union hod carrier for a construction company in Madison, making the good wage of $3.55 an hour. This enabled me to save enough to move my household to Providence, Rhode Island, in time for the fall semester. Late in the summer I was asked to present a seminar on my work to a group of professors and students at the Theoretical Chemistry Institute. I took the day off from construction work and stood at a white board and lectured on quantum mechanics. I had put on a lot of muscle and was deeply tanned, with a white hat line on my forehead from my construction helmet. One friend, a student who was to graduate with the PhD and take a job at the National Bureau of Standards, kindly offered to do whatever he could to help me out after he got to the NBS. I was the one who had not made it.

Brown University and MIT

I bought a 1955 Oldsmobile sedan for $135, a trailer with a canvas cover for $75, and a "universal" trailer hitch from Montgomery Ward, which I bolted to the rear bumper of the car. With this rig I would move my household from Madison to Providence. Whatever did not fit would be left behind. The hitch failed twice: once in Ohio and once just as I turned off the Massachusetts Turnpike to go south to Providence. In both cases the safety chains held, and everything stayed together. But repairs were not possible in Massachusetts because it was 2 AM and no garage was open. I jury-rigged the hitch by wrapping it with the safety chains and managed to limp into Providence at 4 AM. I had been mailed a key to a rental apartment. We gratefully entered our new home and went to sleep. We had made it to Brown University. What I found there was quite wonderful.

In the basement of the Chemistry building was a laboratory with several molecular beam machines built by John Ross' students. Each had its own special purposes and capabilities. The experiments performed on those machines produced data that stimulated theoreticians in the group to work out interpretations. I was now one of those. Similar laboratories in several universities in this country and in Europe were churning out such data and there was a friendly academic competition among them to do the next new thing and to make definitive interpretations. We felt a particularly sharp competition with a laboratory at Harvard. We visited each other's laboratories and attended each other's seminars. It was only a short drive to Cambridge, Massachusetts, where Harvard and MIT sat on the Charles River. John Ross presided over our group with generosity and good humor. He seemed to understand everything. No technical idea seemed to be beyond his grasp. He is one of the very few professors of physical science I have encountered who is equally comfortable with laboratory apparatus and with theory, however complex. For me, it was quite wonderful to be located in a laboratory, where I could see how the observations were made. I had already begun working in quantum mechanical scattering theory at Wisconsin. This equipped me to take on a question that had puzzled scientists for a dozen years or so. John Ross had just the right problem for my PhD thesis.

Several laboratories had observed that, when a beam of alkali metal atoms (for example, potassium, sodium, or lithium) collided with a beam of halide molecules (for example, hydrogen bromide, methyl iodide, or bromine diatomic molecule) the products of reaction were found to go consistently in one direction or another. These were highly reactive, exothermic systems. The alkali halide molecules (potassium bromide, for example) that were formed in those collisions would be found predominantly in the forward direction or backward direction relative to the initial center-of-mass velocity vector of the alkali metal beam. No one knew why this happened. Several attempts had been made to use classical scattering theory to reproduce the experimental results, to no avail. Might it turn out that the phenomenon was quantum-mechanical? Could the quantum mechanical scattering theory developed for nuclear physics be used for these molecular collisions? Could we compute probability density functions (called "differential cross sections") that would exhibit this peculiar directional behavior? Now that you know something of my interest in bringing the methods of mathematical physics to bear on problems in chemistry, you can imagine how delighted I was to get this question. It took two years to get the answer, which was published in my PhD thesis for Brown University. The answer was "yes and yes and yes." Those were an eventful two years.

I settled into my role in John Ross' group and got on with discharging my teaching obligations and a bit of coursework. But the main thing was the thesis. I was helped by Byung Chan Eu, a postdoctoral fellow who was preparing for a career in academia. BC, as he was called, was a fine mathematician, and suggested several steps that helped my work along. After one semester John Ross took a sabbatical in Europe, and BC assumed his role as my advisor *pro tem.* I think this was good for us. It was surely productive. But things were happening that we discovered only later. MIT was calling John Ross to serve as Chairman of their Department of Chemistry. Our little world was being upset. Prof. Ross had secretly returned to Cambridge to discuss the position, and did accept. We found this out when he returned at the end of the semester. He would leave the molecular beam apparatuses at Brown, and those experimentalists working on them would stay. But theoreticians were free to go with him. This was an easy choice for me. We moved our household to an apartment in Watertown, Massachusetts, and my office to the basement of Killian Court, the main building of the Massachusetts Institute of Technology. Above my office, at the crown of the building, were carved the names of great figures from the history of human thought. There was Aristotle, and around the corner, Newton. My office was just below them, so it would be correct to say that I studied under Aristotle and Newton at MIT. I was very much aware of their presence, however silly it might seem to you. I sat at my desk contemplating fluctuations of the vacuum, Dirac's theory of antimatter. Why not? I felt so very lucky. How could I ever deserve professors such as Joe Hirschfelder and John Ross? How could I deserve the privilege of being at MIT? I knew that everyone who knew me would expect me to treasure my opportunity. I surely did.

Ross' office was a first floor suite with a reception room for his secretary and a grand inner office. It was paneled in blonde oak and had a fireplace, but no conference table. It had a large desk, a Persian carpet and several chairs, including a leather easy chair with a hassock. When I met with him at four o'clock on Wednesday afternoons, he would pour us each a small glass of sherry and sit on the hassock, and I would sit on the floor and spread out my papers. The late afternoon light would slant in through the Venetian blinds, and we would do quantum mechanics. You can understand why, behind his back, I called him an angel. He was so very good with his graduate students.

After my thesis was printed and submitted to the faculty of Brown University, the time came for my oral defense. The outside reader chosen by John Ross was Irwin Oppenheim, an MIT faculty member with a high reputation. I drove the fifty-two miles to Brown with a station wagon full of food and drink. This included a fifth of Laphroaig single-malt scotch for the faculty. There were wine and soft drinks for everyone else, and lots of finger food. But nothing would be served unless I passed.

A panel consisting of Ross, Oppenheim and several Brown University Chemistry professors gathered in a third floor conference room, and I had the floor. I was dressed in a dark suit and tie. I took a large piece of chalk and went to the slate blackboard and began to speak. I spoke of alkali metals, covalent halides and Bessel functions. I spoke of the treatment of detector filaments and their sensitivity. I spoke of the puzzle presented by the peculiar angular distribution of the reaction products in molecular beam apparatuses. I spoke of the applicability of nuclear quantum scattering theory to reactive molecular scattering. I spoke of how the kinematical variables appeared in the argument of the Bessel functions in such a way that the angular distributions observed in the laboratory were reproduced. I spoke of the success of what was a relatively simple quantum mechanical treatment of the question. I spoke for ninety minutes. If you had shot me, I would not have felt it. I was loaded with adrenalin. After answering a few questions, I was excused from the room. I went across the hall to the library where the food and drink were ready. I had chalk dust all the way up to my elbow. A short time later John Ross entered the library and extended his hand toward me. He said, "Congratulations, Doctor Huntington."

It was the tradition in the Chemistry Department at Brown University that everyone in the building would be aware when a PhD oral examination was taking place. Everyone knew what to do when the bells rang, which they now did. People piled out of classrooms and offices and came to that third floor conference room. We quickly laid down a tablecloth and put out the food and drink. What a happy moment it was for everyone! The faculty stood over the bottle of scotch until it had been dispatched. They then tottered off to dinner, while we cleaned up and drove back home.

I was now a Doctor of Philosophy.

What Quantum Mechanics Teaches Us

Quantum mechanics works, and it is objectively true. I would add that it is very beautiful. It would be fair to ask what those who use quantum theory actually do. So, here it is: **We compute expectation values and probability density functions.** That is all we do. This is quite different from what one does in classical theoretical physics. In his masterful 1930 book *The Principles of Quantum Mechanics* Paul Dirac wrote:

> The methods of progress in theoretical physics have undergone a vast change during the present century. The classical tradition has been to consider the world to be an association of observable objects (particles, fluids, fields, etc.) moving about according to definite laws of force, so that one could form a mental picture in space and time of the whole scheme. This led to a physics whose aim was to make assumptions about the mechanism and forces connecting these observable objects, to account for their behavior in the simplest possible way. It has become increasingly evident in recent times, however, that that nature works on a different plan. Her fundamental laws do not govern the world as it appears in our mental picture in any very direct way, but instead they control a substratum of which we cannot form a mental picture without introducing irrelevancies.

In this context "substratum" is a metaphysical term. Further, "expectations" and "probabilities" are states of mind.

Because no other words seem to serve, some of the founders of quantum mechanics said that they could not understand quantum mechanics without consciousness, that is, a Mind. In what sense, then, can we say that quantum mechanics is objective? First, **quantum mechanics is empirical.** Its discovery was imposed on us by observations made with the instruments of physical science. Second, **quantum mechanics predicts the results of experiments with very high accuracy.** It is what I call "a discovery of the second kind." These are discoveries that could not have been made by reason alone, but rather are imposed on us by physical observations. Unlike discoveries of the first kind, they at first seem very strange, but gradually become accepted as experimental confirmations come in and ways are found to understand the new knowledge as extensions of what was previously known. There have been a great many such discoveries since the work of Isaac Newton, but we forget how strange they seemed at first, before the new understanding became commonplace. **Quantum mechanics is the greatest of all discoveries of the second kind, but its understanding has never become commonplace.**

The 1887 experiment of Michelson and Morley is a beautiful example of a discovery of the second kind. Since the earth travels on its orbit around the sun at high speed, it was assumed that one would observe a difference in the speed with which light moves if measured in the direction of the orbital motion as compared to the direction toward the sun. Physicists of the time assumed that there must exist a "lumeniferous ether" that carried light waves through space, and this experiment was to reveal its existence for all to see. The measured speed of light traveling in the two directions would surely be different. Michelson and Morley set up a very well thought-out test: they would observe the difference in light speed by the interference of light waves in the two directions. Their instrument is called an interferometer. It was mounted on a slab of granite that floated in a pool of mercury. This would isolate the instrument from vibrations and would allow turning the interferometer to vary the angles relative to the orbital direction. The result? No difference was found between the speeds of light measured in the two directions. It seemed that the lumeniferous ether did not exist, after all. Light did not seem to require a medium in which to propagate. This was stunning. The result has since been confirmed to one part in a hundred million billion. This observation led directly to Einstein's Theory of Special Relativity, published in 1905, which showed that light has only one speed, in any frame of reference. This has since become commonplace knowledge.

Some have said that to understand quantum mechanics one would only need to understand the "two-slit" experiment. I would not say that myself because there are features of quantum theory not revealed by that experiment, but let it do for now. I will describe the experiment operationally. This is appropriate because **quantum mechanics is operational**. In quantum theory the observations of physical science are represented by "operators" which are linear. (The consequences of their linearity are many. Perhaps we will come back to this.) The operators operate on mathematical objects variously referred to as "wave functions," "kets," "wave vectors," or "state functions." A process of mathematical convolution produces the expectation values or probability density functions desired, which predict the results of the experiment. There you have it.

The two-slit experiment consists of a source of a beam of particles, with collimating and analyzing devices that narrow the beam and select the range of velocities or wavelengths of the beam particles, a barrier with two slits, and a screen on which the particles will be manifested as individual spots. The theoretician constructs a "wave packet" that describes the conditions of the beam of particles, whether they be photons or particles with mass. (The treatment is the same because all particle motion is accompanied by a wavelength.) The wave packet is mathematically launched toward the slits and the screen that stands behind it. Now, because we can specify the number of particles in the wave packet, let us say that the wave packet contains only one particle. We can do this because we can set up our laboratory source to only occasionally produce a particle. Consequently, a particle in such a rarefied beam cannot interact with any other particle, but only with the slits, the screen and itself. We watch as the wave packet passes through **both** slits and makes a single spot on the screen. **A wave packet is inherently non-local.** It contains only one particle that could be found anywhere within it. Because of this, the particle's wave packet emerges at the back of the slits as wavelets that interfere with each other, producing an interference pattern on the screen. But our particle produces only one spot, somewhere on the screen. This seems unsatisfying, because the result of our computation was an interference pattern, and we got only one spot. What is going on here? Where did the wave packet go?

If we wait patiently for more particles to make the trip through the apparatus to the screen we will eventually see the interference pattern emerge. We will come to understand that **the interference pattern that we computed predicted accurately the probable** locations of spots on the screen, but it told us nothing at all about where an individual spot would be found.

Second, we must acknowledge that **the interference pattern we observed was produced by particles interfering *with themselves*.**

Third, we are forced to conclude that **a particle's wave packet disappears instantly and everywhere when the spot appears on the screen. The particle's location being known now, the probability associated with the wave packet becomes instantly absurd. This has been demonstrated in several very clever experiments in which two "entangled" particles, participating in a single quantum state, have been observed at once, even though separated by several kilometers. The observation of the state of one such particle has instantaneously determined the state of a second particle, without respect for the distance between them.**

Last, **quantum mechanics teaches us that an estimate of probability can properly refer only to a future event, and never to an event of the past.**

I was among the third generation to learn quantum mechanics. I was quite young and open to learning whatever I found to be trustworthy in physical science. I simply wanted to know what works. Prof. Adam Bincer opened up for me the beautiful general quantum theory of Paul Dirac. I offer the understanding presented here as authoritative, deeply personal, and objective. The controversy over quantum entanglement simply did not concern me until much later in my life. Only later did I spend time reflecting on Albert Einstein's objections to the quantum theory which had been defended by Niels Bohr and definitively presented by Dirac in 1930. In 1935 Einstein and two others published a potential show-stopper, the "EPR Paper." It was based on a particular premise: *"A sufficient condition for the reality of a physical quantity is the possibility of predicting it with certainty, without disturbing the system."* Clearly, Einstein was arguing from a philosophical perspective, and not from an empirical one. This put him in the company of the likes of Plato, in the realm of pure thought. His train of argument led him to the conclusion that quantum entanglement would inevitably occur if quantum theory were correct and "complete." He could not accept this. Nature just could not be that way. But, however powerful one's intuition might seem regarding Nature, observation will trump intuition every time. One simply must be humble before the data. In time, Einstein was proven wrong. See Amir Aczel's excellent account in *Entanglement: The Unlikely Story of How Scientists, Mathematicians, and Philosophers Proved Einstein's Spookiest Theory,* which Einstein himself did not believe.

The Cold War and Ayn Rand

I was always glad to see Yucca Mountain rising up in the distance as I drove north into the Nevada Test Site. I knew that I would soon be inside the mountain, tending to my experiments. My place was there, alongside others engaged in the development of America's strategic nuclear weapons. All of us involved in nuclear weapon testing in those days were mission-driven and certain of the importance of our work. Our battles occurred only in our imaginations, thank God, but they were nonetheless quite vivid to us. Once in a dream I watched as a Soviet missile descended gracefully over San Francisco, incandescent against a pale blue midday sky. I knew what would happen, and I had no time to warn anyone. I knew that everyone within thirty miles would be incinerated, and I was helpless.

I had come to California to join a company called Physics International that had spun off from the Lawrence Livermore National Laboratory to offer Atomic Energy Commission technologies to the Department of Defense. The center of our professional community was the Defense Atomic Support Agency, later called Defense Nuclear Agency. It was charged with serving as the interface between the Department of Defense and the Atomic Energy Commission, performing underground nuclear tests, and conducting research to assure that the new strategic military systems could function as necessary in the intensely hostile environment of a nuclear battle. Our Spartan missile carried a multi-megaton nuclear warhead that was designed to destroy incoming missiles above the atmosphere with X-rays at a range of many miles. The heat of the explosion would be so intense that it would be radiated away as "thermal" X-rays, rushing toward the target at the speed of light, in an expanding spherical shell about a hundred feet thick — megatons of X-rays, if you can imagine it. My specialty was radiation physics, and this was my reality.

At a young age I had been made Director of the Radiation Physics Division of that company. I had little opportunity to use quantum mechanics in that work, but my background in physics, mathematics and chemistry was put to good use. I was twenty-nine years old when I joined that company. Its 300 employees averaged twenty-nine years of age. We thought we were pretty hot. It seemed we could do anything we tried to do. Because of our unique role in the defense community, we got to collaborate with many defense agencies and major contractors. I made it my business to be always right. I am not sure that you would have liked me.

I had come out of my early sadness very much introverted and bookish. That had served me well in the solitary life of scholarship, but it would not do in industry. While still in university I had become captivated by the "Objectivist" philosophy of Ayn Rand. It taught that very capable people, like the heroes of her novels *The Fountainhead* and *Atlas Shrugged*, carried the weight of society on their shoulders because of their radical competence and productivity, and that the socialist forces of their societies, like the Lilliputians, would tie them up to unjustly gain what her heroes had produced. Her economic philosophy was about freely making, and keeping, agreements. The title of her book *The Virtue of Selfishness* says it all. Her ideas were radically anti-Communist.

Now, with executive authority in industry, I put her philosophy to work. I always knew what I wanted out of a meeting, whether or not I had called it. I knew when my objectives had been met and when to stop the talking. I met my financial and technical performance objectives or re-negotiated them in good time. My stuff worked, and I did not conceal my contempt for those at my level who were not so careful or so committed to their promises. The company president openly called me a "Neitzschean superman." This was a bit of a put-down, but was said admiringly. He did not know how I did these things. I will let you in on the secret: You must let people know that you are watching.

When I took over the Radiation Physics Division its finances were a mess. Many of its projects were over budget and behind schedule. Its scientists and support staff were used to doing whatever they wanted to do on a given day. Many of them were twice my age.

I did not sleep well for a while. Then I acted. Because we were operating in an "incurred cost" environment, we all had to fill out weekly time sheets so that our labor hours could be charged to the correct accounts. I interviewed all fifty-five people each week regarding the activities they planned for the following week. I wrote them down. Then I posted them over each of our two coffee stations, with the following text: "I understand that these are your plans for the next week. This is what I expect to see on your time sheets. If your plans change, please let me know in advance." What happened is just what you would expect. Some very sharp graffiti appeared on those notices, apparently written by some of our most mild-mannered scientists. There was grumbling. And then everyone began to comply. This oversight was supplemented with brief monthly project reviews. On one particular day of a month, no project manager was to travel except with special permission. He was to show up with a concise statement of the status of his project. Cost, schedule and technical performance; red, yellow or green. My deputy and a representative of the Contracts Department were with me in the room. There was little discussion of anything green. A yellow or a red would lead to at least one action item with responsible party and due date. Action items were published and due dates were enforced. At the end of the review we would always ask, "What else we can do to help you?" All of the management resources that might be needed were present.

As people got more and more used to this oversight, they began to relax. They watched as our division's business went from red to yellow to green. I continued to make technical contributions to the work, but remained active in management for the remainder of my nearly three decades as a defense scientist. I had had no management education whatever.

Which is why I responded positively to a telephone call from out of the blue. In mid-career I was serving as President of a small company I had founded, Astron Research and Engineering. The phone rang, and I heard a voice saying, "You don't know me. I am the president of a division of TRW here in Silicon Valley. I would like to tell you about an organization I belong to, and to invite you to consider joining." He described an organization known at the time as TEC Worldwide. Its members were chief executive officers who were formed into groups of about a dozen, who met together one day per month. They could not be competitors or suppliers to one another. They served as an ideal, unofficial board of directors for each other. They became friends who were deeply concerned about one another's success and happiness. Their meetings were presided over by a professionally trained "chairman" who visited each of them privately once a month. Most of the group meetings included a three-hour lecture by a specialist in one or another aspect of management. But the heart of the meetings, which members looked forward to most eagerly, was the "executive session," in which several members would present unresolved issues they were facing. The chairman saw to the selection and preparation of those issues, and he saw to it that, after the brief presentations, only clarifying questions could be asked. After those questions had been dealt with it was the common experience that the presenter's own question was re-worded. This wordsmithing was often an eye-opener for the presenter. Only then could members offer their suggestions. After the free discussion, the presenter was asked to commit to a plan of action on his issue. He became accountable to his group for his actions. All this proceeded in deep confidentiality.

I have gone into this in some detail because I did join TEC, and I found it most helpful. Jumping ahead a bit, I will tell you that, after I was ordained an Anglican priest I felt called to do what I could for the spiritual well-being of Silicon Valley executives. I was recruited to serve as the chairman of three TEC groups, a role that I filled for four years. At one time or another I had fifty-two chief executive officers in my care. I was named Canon Missioner to Silicon Valley for my diocese. There is much to tell about all of this. Clearly, something had changed. I had diverged far from Ayn Rand's selfish Objectivism.

I had been softened over time by my life experience. A happy second marriage was the key. And the experience of raising six children, all of whom were different. And the experience of many intense collaborations within the aerospace industry. I worked for many years with highly gifted people who strove to succeed in very challenging work. Deep friendships were formed along the way. Ayn Rand's worldview would no longer do for me. In fact, I had outgrown it long ago.

Earthquake

On Thursday evenings the monks of the Order of the Holy Cross in their white habits joined us for Eucharist followed by dinner in the Refectory. This was a regular event at our seminary. I had just arrived. I watched the monks closely. I was searching for a spiritual director. I finally made an appointment to visit a tall, dignified monk, who seemed to be good natured. So it was that I sat in the study of Fr. Thomas Schultz, the Prior of Incarnation Priory, to ask him to take me on. He said that we would give it a try. I could visit him weekly for eight weeks, then we would see whether we should continue. He asked what brought me to seminary, and I proceeded to tell him. After a short time he stopped me and asked, "Have you written this down?" I answered, "No. I don't want people to think I am crazy." He said, "Write it down!" So I did. A formative experience of my first semester in seminary was writing Fr. Schultz two long single-spaced letters telling the story of my call to the priesthood. The following account draws on those letters and other contemporaneous records, though my memory seems to be quite fresh.

***

Though I had been baptized in the Church of England as an infant, I had not been a churchgoer. Judy and I had raised six children without baptizing them. After ten exhausting years as CEO of a small research company, I had semi-retired to a newly-incorporated company that I owned outright. It was to be my personal practice in aerospace science. I would have professional "associates" as needed for project work, but no employees. This was to be a low overhead, low stress operation. My office was on the seventh floor of a bank building in downtown San Jose, with a view east toward Mount Hamilton.

I had for many years called myself "agnostic." I thought that there was no certain way to know that Christian truth claims, whatever they were, were actually true. I just took a pass and went on with my life. Now our children were all grown and out of the house. Judy and I discussed attending a church. I wanted to learn about what was, after all, my own tradition, and I wanted to participate in a worthy, countercultural and charitable presence in our community. I wanted to contribute. I thought of it like joining a country club. I felt no spiritual need, no spiritual curiosity. Judy chose a handsome carpenter-Gothic church that turned out to be Trinity Cathedral, the cathedral of the Episcopal Diocese of El Camino Real. We arrived early for the principal Sunday service and listened as the choir rehearsed four-part Tudor anthems. This was our kind of music. There was a whiff of incense in the air. The red candle in the sanctuary seemed Catholic. The high redwood ceiling was like the interior of a sailing ship hull, turned upside down. There was beauty all around. Dean Philip Getchell gave a sound sermon. He reminded me of Bing Crosby at his best.

My religious preparation had been scanty. In retrospect, I now think that the Carmelite sisters who taught us at Mount Carmel School in Socorro affected my interior life quite deeply. We students had infinite respect for them. I took Catechism with all the rest, and I attended mass, but this Anglican child could not be confirmed or receive communion. It was there that I learned that a priest was a young man in a black cassock who strode across the quadrangle saying, "Caramba! Caramba!" He seemed to be always angry.

The second time we attended Trinity was Palm Sunday. Dean Getchell announced that an Inquirers' Class would begin the next week for those wishing to know more about Anglicanism. Of course, we signed up. In the first class Dean Getchell taught about the Book of Common Prayer (BCP). I asked, "When was the first Book of Common Prayer published?" He answered, "1549." I asked, "How can I get a copy?" He said, "I have some cloth-bound copies right here for ten dollars." So, I bought two copies. Mine fell open to *A Thanksgiving for the Birth or Adoption of a Child*. It was just beautiful, and quite touching. I found the whole book to be beautiful.

Dean Getchell made us all promise to read one Gospel. He told us that we should start thinking about confirmation, that this was a confirmation class. That Bishop Shimpfky would be with us on Trinity Sunday to perform confirmations. I asked, "When is Trinity Sunday?" He said, "June 6." Gulp. I knew that the question could not be put off to another time. I must decide *now* whether to be confirmed. I opened the BCP to the Confirmation service for the required vows. Here is what I found:

> I would have to renounce evil.

> I would have to make a commitment to follow Jesus as my Savior and Lord.

> I would have to say the Apostles' Creed.

But how could I say these things? I did not fully understand their meaning. And there was so little time. I could not speak falsely. This was about the truth claims of the Christian faith. What were they, after all?

I bought a leather-bound bible and began to read. I read all four Gospels and Acts of the Apostles. I raided bookstores for books on the trustworthiness of the Gospel accounts. I stumbled upon C. S. Lewis' *Mere Christianity*. I read hugely and urgently. I read the Bible at night, in bed. The Bible felt electric in my hands. It was uncomfortable to hold. Tears constantly rolled down my cheeks onto the pillow. Something was happening to me. I knew it would be absurd to ask whether the events related in the Gospels were "likely" to have happened. I knew this from quantum mechanics. The idea of probability simply does not apply to past events. In any event, the improbability of the Gospel accounts would make the evangelists' point: these were miracles. The question I asked was, "If these events actually occurred, would I expect them to be reported pretty much as we see them in the Bible?" My answer was "Yes." In those days there were no journalistic standards. These were accounts of witnesses to miracles, told with the intention of convincing the listener of their truth. I was being asked to surrender.

If this were true, everything would change for me. Everything would be new. I could not turn away.

On May 30, Pentecost, Judy was to be baptized. As we entered the church I told her, "If you want to receive communion after your baptism, I will be at your side." We knelt shoulder to shoulder at the altar rail to receive our first communion together.

Dean Getchell noticed. After the service I said to Dean Getchell that I would like to make an appointment to discuss confirmation. He had an opening the next Tuesday, which was my fifty-fourth birthday.

At the appointed time I entered Dean Getchell's office and sat on the couch. I studied my shoes. I was a businessman. I shined my shoes every morning. So I looked at my shoeshine and said, "I am ready to be confirmed. I have no reservation. If you are not comfortable with this, we can wait for another time." I had surrendered. This was a huge statement for me, and Dean Getchell was aware. He knew of my ignorance and my earnestness. I had not told him about my struggles. Nor had I told Judy. I had approached my problem as I always had as a scholar: alone and in silence. I had not wanted to disrupt our confirmation class with a lot of questions. At this that good and wise man sat back in his chair and said, "John, there is something you do not know about me. I am a golf pro. On my days off I teach golf. I show people how to hit a golf ball. I sometimes reach around them to swing the club together with them. Whatever I do, they eventually catch on. The older I get, the less confidence I have in judging a person's spiritual progress. So, let's go ahead and confirm you. Eventually, you will catch on."

The next Sunday, June 6, 1993, was Trinity Sunday. Bishop Shimpfky sat just above the steps, in an opening in the altar rail to lay hands on the candidates and confirm them, one at a time. I was third in line. I knelt before the Bishop and handed my prayer book to a priest. I had no expectation of any kind. I felt empty. I did not know about *kenosis*, which is spiritual self-emptying.

I was simply offering myself for I knew not what. I folded my hands in prayer and rested my chin on my fingertips. The Bishop placed his hands on my head and I immediately experienced the most extreme violence. His hands struck my head with a high-frequency, rough kind of slapping that seems in retrospect to have been humanly impossible. His voice droned on in a deep, unintelligible basso. I was profoundly comfortable. I watched from above and behind my body. Eventually his voice stopped, and I could not move. He gently raised my head using his crooked index finger under my chin. But my eyes were closed. I was embarrassed. With great effort I opened my eyes. But they were rolled back into my head. I was showing the poor man the whites of my eyes. I was embarrassed. With great effort I rolled my eyes down. But they were focused at infinity, and I still could not see the Bishop. Then, with great effort I managed to focus my eyes on his kindly smile. I did my best to respond, smiling with my eyes. I could not stand up. A priest standing nearby helped me to my feet, and I stood behind the altar rail with the others newly confirmed.

We find in the Book of Common Prayer the words spoken by the Bishop as he laid his hands on me: *Strengthen, O Lord, your servant John with your Holy Spirit; empower him for your service; and sustain him all the days of his life. Amen.*

After all had been confirmed and had gathered behind the altar rail, Bishop Shimpfky stood off to the side and in a jolly way said, "This is a fine confirmation class. I see in this group a couple of priests and maybe even a bishop." At the same time I saw him look directly at me and say wordlessly that I must be a priest. At the word "priest" there was an explosion in my chest—an earthquake of acknowledgement. I was to be a priest. All of my life now made sense for the first time, back to the beginning. In that instant I received a commission: my life from this moment forward was to comfort people and to bring them hope. It was clear. There could be no doubt. This was almost unbearably sweet.

We then went to the pews for the rest of the mass. I noticed an unusual gracefulness in my body. It seemed that I could not be clumsy if I tried. My voice was deeper and more resonant than I had ever experienced. My chest felt strangely inflated. This sensation persisted for several weeks. At the announcements I took the microphone briefly to say that I had just turned fifty-four, and that it seemed that my life would hold further adventures.

After the mass I went to the choir to invite Ada May Ames to brunch. She had sponsored me for confirmation. Helen Williams, who sat next to her in the choir, looked at me and said, "Well John, it seems that you will be turning your collar around." She was the wife of Canon Douglas Williams, a senior priest at the Cathedral. She had grown up in the church, and was very knowledgeable. She *knew* that I would be a priest. It was two years later, after my first year in seminary, before I dared to ask her what she meant by that comment. She said that when I knelt before the Bishop and he laid his hands on me, the air seemed filled with electricity, and it was clear to her that I would be a priest. Her observation has been a comfort to me ever since.

***

On Monday I flew to Albuquerque for a classified conference on strategic missile defense. Tuesday morning I ordered breakfast and sat, looking at the floor, not eating. The waitress became concerned. "Are you all right?" I was going to be a priest.

After being badged and seated in the conference hall, I became agitated. I shot up from my seat and half ran to my hotel room. I closed the door, sat on the edge of the bed and burst into great, wracking sobs. I promised that Charlie would never be forgotten. I promised that Mother, who was in an assisted living facility with stage III Alzheimer's, could come home to live with us. And I promised that I would "follow where this leads." All three promises were clearly being asked of me.

I found Charlie's grave in a local cemetery there in Albuquerque, brushed off his modest stone, knelt on the grass, burst into tears and made the same three promises.

I had a meeting scheduled for two o'clock in the afternoon on Friday of that week at the Los Alamos National Laboratory. LANL owed our little company a lot of money, and I was there to collect. I had a record of two years of telephone calls that had not been returned. I was staying at a motel in the small town of Española, where, after breakfast I sat in the sun with my Bible to kill time. Next after Acts of the Apostles was Romans. I did not know that this was Paul's theological summation—that it is considered complex and subtle. I just read it. It seemed so clear. It was as though every word had been written just for me.

At 2 PM I was ushered into the Administration building and seated at the end of a very long conference table. Everyone else remained standing. They seemed to be very ill at ease. They had looked into the matter and discovered their liability. One of their contract administrators had prematurely closed out a prime contract with the Department of Defense, on which we had been a subcontractor. He had not waited to collect all of the costs, which should have included our final invoice. They had made a mistake. They could not go back for more money, since the contract was closed. Would I give them a copy of the telephone log showing two years worth of unreturned calls? I did not want to embarrass them. I declined. But they persisted, and I let them make a copy. They continued to talk in my presence. They could identify a source of funds. It would have to come out of Laboratory Director's discretionary account. They thought they could find enough. What was I going to do? I answered that I would send them a letter demanding full payment by July 1. (This was already June 11.) If I received payment by July 1, that would be the end of the matter. If I did not receive payment by that date I would turn the matter over to a lawyer. Interest and collection costs would be added. They seemed very relieved. I sent the letter and they sent the money. I had never been in a meeting like that one. I was so much at peace in the midst of their agitation.

It was now Saturday morning and I was back home in San Jose. I had to tell Judy that I was going to be a priest. I found her sitting in the sun room with a dog on her lap. I stood in the doorway and started to talk. I did not know how to do this. After my first attempt, she said, "Oh, the Bishop was talking to those young kids, not to you." I tried again. She could see that something was going on. She suddenly stopped me and said, "John, the Holy Spirit clearly has you by the throat. You are going to be a priest!"

Just like that. She has never since wavered. What a blessing she is to me.

Now I had to tell Dean Getchell. At the Sunday coffee hour I asked him for an appointment. He had an opening on Tuesday. I carefully rehearsed what I would say to him. I again took my place on his couch, and he in his desk chair. I again studied my shoeshine. He said, "Well, John, what can I do for you?" I responded, "Father, after the confirmations last week, did the Bishop address me directly and say with conviction that I must be a priest?" He said, "A *priest*?!" He about fell out of his chair. But he saw that I was miserable. He became my pastor in that moment. This was a serious and tender business, however surprising. He knew his responsibility. I did not know this, but he did. There would be all the time in the world to confirm a vocation, but his responsibility was clear. He would take me to the Bishop. That would be the first canonical step toward ordination. He said, "You have to talk to the bishop. I will make an appointment." I said, "Couldn't you just ask him if he meant it?" I had only met the Bishop once, on that Trinity Sunday. He answered, "No, you need to talk to him. I will give him a call and see what we can set up." He then sent me the following note.

Saturday

Dear John,

Just a note to tell you I spoke to the Bishop regarding your query to me about Priesthood. He'd be very glad to see you when he can, but may not be in San Jose 'til after July. So let's think about August or so and stay in touch about it.

Have a wonderful Montana adventure!

In Christ,

Phil Getchell

July was Dean Getchell's month off. It turned out that August was the Bishop's month off. Evidently I was to have time to cool off a bit. I stewed in my juices those two months.

My family by now knew about my experience of a call to the priesthood. I was candid with everyone that this was not my idea. That I had not cooked it up in the way one decides to become a lawyer or a veterinarian. This was different, and I was in earnest. But I did experience waves of uncertainty. I tried my best to expose the nonsense and get back to my life, as I said to myself. I constructed a number of hypotheses. Had the Bishop hypnotized me? Did I have some unworthy delusions of grandeur? Was I trying to puff myself up? Did I just imagine things? I examined every hypothesis worth the name, and all failed. I kept coming back to the same conclusion: This was something that happened *to* me. A will other than my own was at work in my life. Then, at some point along the way I came upon a show-stopper. There was no way I could ever be the good person I would have to be to become a priest. I would have to decline. I observed my behavior and I was appalled. I spent a week fishing in Montana with several male relatives, including my three sons. I was shocked at what I observed. My rough humor was often at the expense of others, especially my sons. This was very painful to me. But this all changed at about 2

AM as I lay in my bedroll, staring at the ceiling of my tent. I would have to make changes to my habitual behavior whether or not I pursued ordination. I could no longer use this as an excuse not to go forward. I was all in now.

The first day of September is the traditional start of dove season. A friend phoned to propose that we drive to Coalinga the prior evening to camp in a creek bed and shoot doves in the morning. For some reason I declined. I decided to hang around. The first of September fell on a Wednesday. I got a phone call from Dean Getchell about 9 AM. The Bishop was back from vacation. Wednesday was his office day at the Cathedral. He had an opening at 11 AM. Would I like to meet with him? "Yes!" I was ready now. I went early and sat to wait in the library. The Dean passed by and said, "Oh, John, you are here. Let me see if the Bishop is in his office." It turned out that the Bishop had gone to Laurel's Delights, a coffee shop around the corner. The Dean said, "Let's go." So I followed the Dean through the parking lot and around the corner to Laurel's Delights to talk with the Bishop about priesthood. It seemed unreal.

We could see through the plate glass window that the bishop was in conversation with a woman over coffee. We went in and they stood up. The Bishop said "We are just finished. But let's stay. I could use another coffee." I said, "Here? In this public place?" The Bishop said, "We can sit over by the window. It will be private enough." Dean Getchell ordered a double mocha for me, a decaf for himself and an espresso for the Bishop. Thus caffeinated, I began to speak. I poured out my heart. I spoke for about an hour, only occasionally interrupted by a question from the bishop. I spoke about how my background might be helpful to the church. That I had been very much a part of the business scene in Silicon Valley. That I spoke the languages of business and physical science. That I could perhaps reach people who are not otherwise reached by the church. That I was very much concerned for the spiritual well being of the people outside the walls of the church. That I would learn quickly and well, in spite of my current ignorance.

There was a pause, and then the Bishop spoke. He said, "I have the authority to do this. John, effective today I am placing you in the ordination process for this diocese. I will send you a letter to that effect. Dean, get John busy on a project. John, have your papers in to the diocese by the first Sunday of Advent." I was astonished. I had not expected this.

I could not work the rest of the day. I puttered around doing chores. I told a sympathetic shop owner that I had just met with my priest and my bishop, and it seemed that I might some day become a priest in the Episcopal Church. He said, "That is happening a lot these days."

The next day, September 2, I had business in Santa Barbara. I was flying my plane somewhere near Paso Robles just after sunrise, on autopilot. I found myself in fervent prayer, with heaving chest and tears, committing myself to God to be his priest.

Mother and Charlie in Silver City.
September 1943.

Here I am in Socorro in 1944.

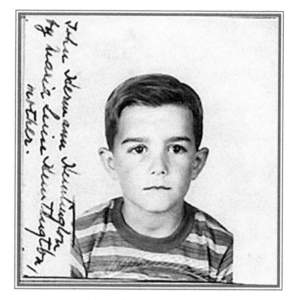

In 1945, after Charlie's death.

High school senior, age 16.

Cold war scientist, age 35.

First mass as an Anglican priest, with Deacon Nancy Partanen.

Christian Century

Missionary priest in Silicon Valley.

Noella Levy

With the Community of Joseph.

Rector of St. Andrew's Church in Cripple Creek,
with Judy.

The Church Divinity School of the Pacific

I now began my conversation with Holy Scripture, the Christian saints and mystics, and the Church itself. I was in pursuit of the truth. I would follow where it led me. It helped very much to admit my total ignorance.

I stood in the pews after a noon mass and asked Canon Williams for his help. Would he serve as my spiritual director to help me prepare for seminary? I said, "I don't know what I am doing." I was crying. He said, "Yes, I will do it. But there will be no guarantees." "I will ask the Bishop whether you would be acceptable." He smiled and said, "That should not be a problem." Canon Williams was an examining chaplain for the diocese, highly intellectual, and a perfect choice.

Thus began an intense year of preparation. My task was to become familiar with the entire Bible and the Book of Common Prayer. I was to be free to raise any question in complete safety. Perhaps it was from my experience with the Carmelite sisters in Socorro that I was predisposed toward the Catholic worldview. It helped that Canon Williams was Anglo-Catholic. He had begun his university studies in physical science, but had changed to philosophy and theology. I was the scientist that he had once wanted to be, and he was the theologian that I might become. We formed a deep friendship. We met once a month for three hours, in the Bishop's office at the Cathedral. I would bring with me the stack of books I had been reading, and I would bring my questions. During that year I served at the altar as a sub-deacon and became a "sacristy rat." I purchased my first alb, which hung in the sacristy. At the end of the year Canon Williams released me to find another spiritual director in seminary. My new life was beginning.

I purchased an Anglican cassock from England, and I was off to seminary. "Holy Hill" sits just north of the University of California in Berkeley. The Graduate Theological Union there is a consortium of nine seminaries that consolidated their libraries in 1969. The Flora Lamson Hewlett Library, which holds this remarkable theological collection, sits just across Ridge Road from the Church Divinity School of the Pacific (CDSP), the seminary of the Episcopal Church in which I enrolled in the summer of 1994. Three of the adjacent seminaries are Catholic. A Lutheran seminary sits on top of a hill a mile or so away, with a fine view of San Francisco Bay. I was now a seminarian. I quickly found the GTU Bookstore, just the other side of the CDSP campus. I surely would not lack resources for my theological study.

***

On a fine August day Judy and I visited CDSP to register, pay the tuition, and arrange for housing. The Administrative Vice President of the seminary showed us the apartment we would occupy, which was handsome and spacious. On the way back to the main campus he said something remarkable, for which I was completely unprepared. He said, "Everyone here seems to be angry. I just do not understand why all the students here are angry." I soon discovered what he was talking about.

During an orientation tour of the seminary led by a second-year student named Nancy I got an eye opener. All the first-year students in our group were women, except for me. Women had been approved for ordination in the Episcopal Church eighteen years earlier, in 1976. At the end of the tour we took seats at a table in the Refectory to chat. The women did the chatting, while I sat and listened. They seemed eager to share a sense of injustice toward themselves as women. All seemed aggrieved over one thing or another. They were all angry. There was no anger in me. I just sat there. Then the matter of the fair linen came up. These are the linens that cover the altar and hang down gracefully at the sides. They need special care. They are made of true linen, the cloth of the flax fiber, which seems to wrinkle if one just looks at it. It seemed that it was always women who had to care for the fair linen. Nancy leaned over the table, looked directly at me and asked, "John, would you do the fair linen this year?" I said "Yes," not knowing what I was getting into. So it was that I would wash those large linens with bleach, hang them on hangers in the doorways of my apartment until they were partly dry, press them dry with two passes through Judy's ElnaPress, and roll them with tissue paper onto cardboard tubes. I would stride through the campus with one or two of them under my arm to deliver them to the sacristy, where I liked to hang out anyway. I called myself "Fair Linen Johnny." I was a sacristan, who cared for the vestments and vessels and instructed the celebrants on special features of the particular services. I sang in the *Schola Cantorum.*

There was also the matter of the urinals in the women's dormitory restrooms. Since women had been accepted into seminary and began to displace men, they had inherited some of the dormitory space, complete with urinals. This apparently angered some of the women. I was told that they planted flowers in them, but I cannot testify to this personally.

Then there was Bill Countryman, our Professor of Greek and New Testament. He introduced himself to us as "gay and not presently partnered." He was a divorced priest with a teenage daughter. He often celebrated mass. He chanted beautifully and preached on homosexuality. At least, it seemed to me that he always worked that subject into his homilies. I was alarmed that this might alienate one particular, rather conservative member of my class. That young man would be a fine priest, and I did not want the church to lose him. I thought it was risky and unkind to keep bringing up homosexuality in the way Countryman was doing. After all, he was a priest, and every priest must be, in the first place, a kind person. Surely he would be sensitive to potentially offending a seminarian. I asked to see him after a mass at which he had given the homily. I did not tell him why I wanted to talk. He said, "Come to my office." I followed him to his office and sat in a chair. I had no chance to say anything before he stood over me and yelled: "You are challenging me! You cannot tell me what to preach." I said, "But Father, surely you don't mean to be unkind. It seems unkind to preach aggressively on homosexuality the way you do." He yelled some more and I was excused. A professor in the next office heard the exchange and clucked sympathetically. I had risked being thrown out of seminary to protect a friend.

There was a war going on in that seminary. On the one side was our Dean Charles Perry. On the other side was Bill Countryman. Dean Perry was a distinguished senior priest who had served successfully as Provost of the National Cathedral in Washington, DC. He had been an effective fundraiser for the cathedral and it was hoped that, among other things, he would do the same for CDSP. But he was a traditionalist. He would not approve homosexual couples sharing a seminary apartment reserved for married seminarians. This would happen only over his dead body. Countryman's response was to dial up the unpleasantness to the point that Dean Perry decided to retire. He was done with strife. Countryman had won. The academic handbook was soon changed to allow cohabiting homosexual couples to live in seminary apartments.

These were the two sources of the anger that the poor Administrative Vice President had sensed.

***

The anger and sense of hurt that I found in my seminary was doing serious damage in the wider church. Most conservatives in the Church had always held that:

- The Church cannot ordain women.
- The Church cannot condone adultery.
- The Church cannot condone homosexual behavior.

These prohibitions were considered by some to be unfair, even cruel. There is something to that argument, of course. But are they unjust? Laws, whether secular or religious, are meant to serve justice. **Equating justice with fairness is a fallacy** that has been exploited recently with great success in some Western societies. The purpose seems always to obtain permission, or license, for some behavior that was previously prohibited. Confusion on this point has led to the wrecking of the Episcopal Church. Otherwise clear-headed people have allowed themselves to be co-opted by permissive agendas through their weakness, which is their need to think of themselves as fair. To regain our balance we might try to remember our many celibate friends who have sacrificed their personal lives for our benefit.

***

During my time in seminary I focused on Sacramental Theology. I needed to make sense of my experience on that Trinity Sunday. I could no longer deny that God is active in the world, in the sacraments, and in my life. I needed urgently to discover whether it could be possible to reconcile priesthood with my grounding in physical science. My love of truth could better be called a passion. I was a careful person, and I had plunged into seminary with certain things unresolved. What better place to work these things out? Seminary was like a three-year retreat, with all the resources of the GTU at my disposal. Characteristically, I took on the problem alone.

I began with physical science. I had to define it. I needed to say what it is, and define its scope and its limitations. I settled on the following definition: **Physical science is the body of knowledge that is based on measurements made by instruments of observation. It is empirical and severely objective.** Next, it is fundamentally pixelized. Apparently continuous data, when examined closely, could always be seen to consist of discrete bits that could be displayed on time-dependent pixels. The retinas of our eyes contain discrete rods and cones that send raw data to our brains for processing into apparently continuous images. The raw data could, with arbitrary accuracy, be displayed on pixels. The key here is the recognition that, whatever instrument we consider, this observation holds. Therefore, **the essential content of physical science, being its raw data, could be displayed with arbitrary accuracy on pixels**. Next, **the raw data are all quantities**. Whatever an instrument measures, it receives its data on a sensor that produces a quantitative signal. Colors, for example, can be broken down into wavelengths or frequencies, and so on. The work of physical science is to make sense of the raw data by some kind of analysis, which treats of possible relationships among sets of quantitative data. For this purpose we employ mathematics.

The instruments of observation can always be described completely. A scientist conceived an instrument, had drawings made, and had it built. Its dimensions and physical attributes, along with their tolerances or uncertainties, are therefore all known. Therefore, **an instrument of physical observation and all the data it collects can be fully described in human language, including mathematics.** In the sense of a Venn diagram, physical science is encompassed completely within the scope of human language. Next, **our human languages are capable of conveying truths that are not accessible to physical science.** We have only to think of our interior lives of meaning, value and purpose to see that this is so.

But language has its limits. However limitless its expressive potential might seem, it has limits. Even when words are sung, or poems read well, there are limits. **There are truths that our minds can grasp that cannot be fully expressed in language.**

Further, **I have found no one who would say that everything that is true can be grasped by the human mind.** We have by this train of thought obtained a nested Venn diagram of our perception of reality that can be expressed in the negative.

All that is true cannot be grasped by the mind.
All that can be grasped by the mind cannot be put into words.
All that can be put into words cannot be measured.

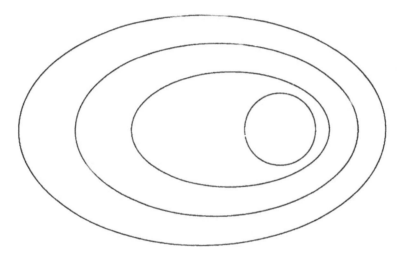

The Venn diagram as I first drew it in seminary.

Proceeding outward beginning with the circle, we have:

- The limit of physical science
- The limit of language (including mathematics)
- The limit of the human mind
- Everything else

We can see that the power of physical science, which comes from its severe objectivity, is also the source of its limitations. These are two sides of one coin.

***

What is a "person?" Some time after my ordination I addressed this question in a class I was teaching in the Religious Studies Department of Santa Clara University. Every day before my class gathered I set the small, articulated wooden figure of a man on my desk, with its arms upraised and its face lifted toward heaven. It was one of those little figures that art students use.

To my class it represented a "person." The subject of the class was the interior life of a person as he or she strives to be productive and peaceful while experiencing the indignities and temptations that inevitably occur when collaborating in an organization of any kind. We brought together the Judeo-Christian wisdom tradition and the best practices offered by our top business schools to consider how best to deal with the practical and spiritual challenges of collaborating in work. The course was titled *Spirituality and Organizational Life*. It was designed to be taken for credit in both Religious Studies and Business in Jesuit universities. Today I would rename it simply *Collaboration*. That little wooden figure was a presence in the classroom. It aroused tender feelings in all of us for reasons that we never articulated. It worked in our hearts and minds without a word being said.

Blank spaces sometimes speak volumes. There is a blank space in the *Oxford Dictionary of Psychology* where the word *per-*

son belongs. There is no entry there, though *person* is used in definitions of some other terms. In the *Penguin Dictionary of Psychology* we find the following: "Psychology, in one guise or another, concerns itself with entities that behave, act, think and emote and do so within the context of some social and physical environment. When such an entity is a member of the species *Homo sapiens* the term *person* is appropriately used as a label." So, *person* is a "label" that can be applied to an "entity."

I give you an exercise. Climb up a mountain and sit on a rock for the day. Spend the day contemplating why the editors of the Oxford dictionary did not dare to define *person* and why the editors of the Penguin dictionary made such a poor attempt at it. I would prefer the blank space to silly nonsense. The word *person* conveys a whole palette of deeply held feelings to us. When we fall in love, it is with a *person*, not a "label" or an "entity." Better the blank space. Our little wooden man filled that blank space in our classroom, and in doing so he touched our hearts.

I asked my class whether anyone knew identical twins. A pretty young woman in the back of the room raised her hand and said, "I dated an identical twin." I asked, "Could you tell them apart?" She blushed deeply and the class tittered. Of course she could tell them apart. She would surely know which of the twins was with her on a date. My question seemed silly and embarrassing.

Then another young woman raised her hand and said, "I *am* an identical twin." I asked, "Can you tell yourselves apart?" The class sat in shocked silence. Most of us have known identical twins, but few have had the experience of *being* an identical twin. But we do know from our own experience that identical twins, as much as they might have in common, are different persons, even though they are genetic clones. Each of them must experience in his own way the mystery of his personal identity, as we all must. But, why does all this seem so embarrassing? In *I Asked for Wonder*, Rabbi Abraham Joshua Heschel put his finger on it:

> *How embarrassing for man*
> *to be the greatest miracle on earth*
> *and not understand it!*
> *How embarrassing for man*
> *to live in the shadow of greatness*
> *and to ignore it,*
> *to be a contemporary of God*
> *and not to sense it.*
> *Religion depends on what man does*
> *with his ultimate embarrassment.*

Irenaeus of Lyon, who is honored as the first Catholic theologian, wrote around the year 180 A.D.: "For the glory of God is a living man; and the life of man consists in beholding God." This is a literal translation from the Latin. The original Greek has been lost. But the sense of what he wrote is clear, and I find that the free translation that we often see is faithful to his meaning: "The glory of God is a human person fully alive."

We are born into relationships with God and with one another. This is what I call Mach's Principle of the Person: **We can hardly be said to exist except as we are reflected in one another's eyes, and in the eyes of God.** This is not something that the editors of those dictionaries of psychology could deal with. And, without this understanding, they could come up with nothing but nonsense. It is embarrassing.

I was sitting in my study at seminary when this Principle of the Person became clear to me. I began to read the Christian saints and mystics with new eyes. Surely, Evelyn Underhill was a Christian mystic. In her landmark 1911 book *Mysticism* she noted that she had found two distinguishing characteristics of all Christian mystics: that they were sensitively aware of the mystery of their unique being, and that this awareness prepared them for, and enabled, their relationship with God. They walked in lively awareness of the presence of the God who knew them in their mothers' wombs and who breathed life into their nostrils. If this definition of mystic suffices, then I conclude that our church pews are filled with mystics, and I must be one of them.

I was being prepared to ascend the pulpit and preach to people gathered in church. This is a terrifying prospect. In the pulpit and at the altar I would be serving *in persona Christi*. This takes one's breath away. More accurately, we must rely on God the Holy Spirit to fill our lungs with breath so that we might give voice to the faith. We would be given the needed breath. We would step off a cliff in faith to receive unfailingly the grace of God to serve his people, every time we stood at the altar or in the pulpit. I wanted to surrender to this intelligently. I visited my favorite professor, Louis Weil, with a question: "What would it be like to be in the presence of Jesus of Nazareth? What would be the effect of his speaking?" He said, "John, write this down: *Ecclesiastical Authority and Spiritual Power in the Church of the First Three Centuries*, by Hans von Campenhausen." This book was written by that scholar after a quarter century of considering my question. Von Campenhausen noted that "spiritual power" is represented in the New Testament by the two Greek words, *dunamis* and *exousia*. The root meaning of *dunamis* is "effective ability." The root meaning of *exousia* is "authority" in the sense of the author of a book. Jesus spoke as one with authority. This kind of authority comes from within. Both *dunamis* and *exousia* are non-coercive forms of supernatural spiritual power, and they are self-authenticating. This gave me a new understanding of what it is to serve *in persona Christi*. We rely on the Holy Spirit to fill the lungs of a priest serving at the altar or in the pulpit, supplying him with the necessary effective ability and authority. Above all, of course, a priest must be a person of deep faith.

In my third year at CDSP in Louis Weil's class on *Holy Orders in Anglicanism*, I faced a dilemma. I was uncomfortable with the idea that I was in some way special. I had expected to find seminarians with stories like mine, but I found none. I had continued to struggle to understand what had happened to me that Trinity Sunday. This was my lodestar—the focus of my inquiry into Sacramental Theology. I asked Prof. Weil whether I should write my term paper in a workmanlike way about a rather straightforward subject, or whether I should take on the interpretation of my experience of call to the priesthood. That wise man replied, "What would be more helpful to you?" I could not dodge the issue now. Because Weil knew something of my story, he gave me a paper published in1974 by Godfrey Diekmann, a Benedictine monk, a Catholic priest, and a well-known professor of Sacramental Theology. Its title was, *The Laying On of Hands: The Basic Sacramental Rite*. It concluded that the central action in all the sacraments is manual, and in all cases the intention was to confer the Holy Spirit. This practice goes back to the beginning of the Church. I concluded that what I had experienced was neither common nor entirely rare: the intention of the sacrament of Confirmation had been effectively accomplished, and I had been drawn into the Church. I had wanted to own the Tradition by learning everything I could about it, but the Tradition now possessed me. I felt a wave of relief. I was one among many now, and I could relax.

My seminary had by now written to Bishop Shimpfky recommending my ordination, but one obstacle stood in the way: Pope Leo XIII's papal bull of 1896, *Apostolicae curae* that declared Anglican Holy Orders "absolutely null and utterly void." My inherent respect for authority made it impossible for me to ignore Pope Leo's words. I had to do the hard work to find out whether they would be decisive for me. If they were, I would have to decline Anglican ordination. If I found them to be questionable, I would, as a mere seminarian, have found myself in disagreement with the successor to Peter. I would be an example of disobedience. I found the account of that papal document in John Jay Hughes' book *Absolutely Null and Utterly Void: An Account of the 1896 Papal Condemnation of Anglican Holy Orders* to be a good help. Hughes had been ordained an Episcopal priest and was later conditionally ordained a Catholic priest. He had done research on the two Episcopal bishops who ordained him deacon and priest and found that they had, in fact, participated in the Apostolic Succession. This is the unbroken chain of bishops, going back to the first apostles, who were consecrated by the laying on of hands by a preceding generation of bishops. Thus, the Church could claim a continuity of God's grace going all the way back. This grace was the gift of the particular spiritual powers appropriate to a bishop, including the power to ordain. While studying in Rome, Hughes asked the Vatican authorities whether in view of his research, his Anglican orders were, in fact, valid. The Vatican responded with a letter in French stating, "There can be no question of a simple recognition of the orders received, with subsequent permission to exercise the priesthood. The church can only require a certain period of studies, at the end of which conditional re-ordination would be granted; but there is no reason why this would be refused, provided the other conditions mentioned [the normal criteria for ordination] were satisfied." (This text is provided in Hughes' much later autobiography, *No Ordinary Fool: A Testimony to Grace*.) To ordain a priest twice is considered to be an offense against God, but conditional ordination would avoid offending God, since its purpose would only be to repair any defect in the first ordination. In our long discussions in Bishop Shimpfky's office, Canon Williams and I had agreed that we fondly hoped for corporate reconciliation between the Anglican churches and Rome, perhaps in our lifetime. In the meantime we could hope for conditional ordination of Anglican priests on a case-by-case basis.

The other objection to Anglican orders made by Pope Leo referred to defects in intention and form of the Anglican Rite of Ordination. I examined the text of the rite that would be used in my ordination and I found no such defect. Any defect in that rite from the early days of the Church of England had long ago been repaired. Also, since the stinging words of Leo were published in 1896, the Anglican churches had taken care to repair any possible defect in the Apostolic Succession. This is why a bishop is consecrated by the laying on of hands by three bishops.

In 1996, the centenary of *Apostolicae Curae*, I had attended the Ecumenical Institute at General Theological Seminary in New York, representing my diocese. A book had been published for the occasion, *Anglican Orders: Essays on the Centenary of Apostolicae Curae 1896-1996*, edited by R. William Franklin. It contains the English text of *Apostolicae Curae* and the English text of *Saepius Officio*, the response of the Archbishops of Canterbury and York. It troubles me to this day that Pope Leo gave no warning to them that *Apostolicae Curae* would be published, declaring their orders to be "absolutely null and utterly void." This lack of courtesy seems inexplicable in a church deeply concerned with the dignity of every human person. The first mark of such concern must surely be courtesy.

I decided to go ahead with my ordination. I would receive the spiritual powers of a priest, or not.

Obedience

Sometimes, as we see in the lives of the saints, some event stopped a person in his tracks and permanently changed the focus of his life — I think of Julian of Norwich as one example among many — and sometimes a kind of growing awareness had reached the point where a person simply had to acknowledge that his worldview had somehow changed. In either case, everything seems new to such a person. When the sacraments occupy a central place in that new worldview it would be proper to call it Catholic. To such a person it is never vain to seek to know God's will. Such a person is rather drawn into a life of prayerful discernment, with its many consolations. It is a life of obedience, which is radically countercultural. My own conversion was sudden and disorienting, so perhaps you can understand the sense of gratitude with which I came upon the following three sentences in *Sacramentum Mundi*, the Catholic theological encyclopedia: ***Obedience consists in the determination to accomplish the will of God in all things. It is a general virtue and the foundation of all the moral virtues. Such obedience makes a person actualize his own being, for the root of action is freedom exercised in commitment to one's fellow human beings and to God.*** Because these words are so valuable to me I framed them and gave them a place of honor in my study. We could expand this concise text to fill a book, but let me just give some hints about where they would lead us.

First, obedience is not passive, but is a "determination to accomplish." This would be nonsense if one lacked confidence that God's will could be discerned. The word *discernment* has a particular meaning in Jesuit parlance. It represents the Jesuit way of thinking and decision-making through contemplation and prayer. Because the discernment process is intended to lead to confident action, Jesuits refer to themselves as "contemplatives in action." This leads to consolation and peace of mind as one makes one's way through life.

Second, obedience is our response to receiving the grace of the theological virtues of faith, hope and charity. In this sense obedience to God can be understood as foundational to the moral life. Our discernment of God's will therefore takes place in the exercise of those theological virtues, which are given by God and orient us toward God.

Third, our self-understanding is shaped and made concrete in the living of this kind of life. The mystery of our being is not in any way diminished, but it is given meaning and made actual by the way we use our freedom. And it is only in truly living for others — for God and our fellow human beings — that we become who we are.

The saints of old, and the saints of our own time, add that we must treasure those who are despised. Mother Teresa of Calcutta exemplified this for us. It seems that everyone knows her story. She has truly touched our hearts. While priests have their particular role of confessors, all of us share in some way a vocation to the care of souls. We cannot know in advance when a person in physical or spiritual need will look to us for sustenance of some kind. But we can notice them. We can turn toward them. We can be fully present to them. And we can be sure that we are doing these things freely in obedience to God's will.

Saint Cuthbert and Saint Ignatius

On a visit to England in the autumn of 1997, driving north toward Scotland, Judy and I diverted to Durham Cathedral. This was a purposeful and urgent detour. I needed to spend time with Saint Cuthbert. His remains are buried beneath the altar of that great cathedral. I had business with him. I was now a transitional deacon, obedient as always, and ignorant of the purposes for which I had been called to the priesthood. At some point it must become clear to me why I had been called. I knew that I was to comfort people and bring them hope, but why flag down a physical scientist who was not causing any trouble? Why not someone else? Why me? I needed clarity. I would soon be ordained a priest.

One cannot distinguish an Anglican deacon from an Anglican priest by his street clothing. The dress is identical. In this instance I was wearing a Roman collar, black shirt, pants and shoes, and a salt-and-pepper tweed jacket. I looked for all the world like an English gentleman priest. We found the nave and sanctuary of the Cathedral closed for cleaning. The women collecting admission fees declined to charge us admission, but opened the rope to let me pass. I made my way behind the altar to the prie dieu over Cuthbert's tomb and knelt in prayer with a question. "Why was I called? Surely there must be a reason that would explain it. It must at some point become clear to me. Help me to understand." The cleaning women were dusting and sweeping the area around me, making sideways glances in my direction. When would I be done so they could finish? In time I got up and rejoined Judy for the drive to Edinburgh.

Cuthbert touched my heart. You could read about him in the Venerable Bede's *Life of Cuthbert*. Should you do that, you would learn why I was attracted to that holy man. He was a monk, a priest, an abbot, a hermit and a bishop, mostly in the area of the Holy Island of Lindisfarne, on the northeast coast of England. He died in the year 687. His strong faith and simple piety, his generous heart and his presence affected people deeply and drew many into a lively Christian faith. I went to him, hoping for clarity regarding my particular vocation. It might make a good story if I could say that I instantly received the clarity I wanted. But I can say that my request was not denied. Clarity came as my experience as a priest unfolded over the next few years. It led me to Saint Ignatius of Loyola. I came to call him "Father Ignatius." I was always filled with happiness when I saw his image. Here is the story.

My pastoral heart was given over to caring for the sick and caring for all the people in the intense work environment of Silicon Valley who had stepped onto a treadmill without thinking things through. After my ordination I returned to the business world as a TEC chair. I agreed to serve in that role because I considered the work to be pastoral even though it was secular, and I believed that it would be at least congruent with my new vocation as a priest. Evenings and weekends I served in a parish, and weekdays I was on the road, tending to my flock. Over the next four years I became deeply involved in the lives of fifty-two Silicon Valley CEOs. For me Silicon Valley went from Petaluma in the north to Monterey in the south. Several of my members had offices in San Francisco. Parking a car there was such a challenge that I ended up using a motorcycle, which I often parked on the sidewalks. Somehow I managed to avoid getting a single parking ticket.

Who were these people, and what kind of companies did they run? On the whole they were highly gifted and deeply committed to their work, and they loved the complexity and the challenges of their role as CEO. To my mind the best of them were "happy warriors" in that they let their joy show. They truly loved the sport of it all. With hardly any exception, they had a balanced approach toward money. But only a few consistently got adequate, regular rest and exercise. About a quarter of them had a business degree. Seven were women. Four of the companies were publicly traded. Twelve of the companies were backed by venture capitalists. Two companies were not for profit. One was foreign owned. Two were subsidiaries of major corporations. About half were privately owned by groups of founders. And their lines of business were very diverse, indeed. Here is the list:

- Technical publishing
- Industrial equipment
- Education
- Packaged foods
- Hydroponic flower production
- Scientific instruments
- Financial services
- Proprietary optics
- Public relations
- Engineering and scientific services
- Chemical equipment
- Mental health care
- Advertising
- Genetics services
- Cancer treatment

- Document storage and destruction
- Nutritional supplements
- Sports equipment
- Construction
- Promotional goods
- Engineering software
- Pathology practice software
- Specialty electronics
- Semiconductor production capital equipment
- Medical services
- Motorcycle sales and service
- Film products
- Nonprofit management services
- Fulfillment-by-mail services
- Game software
- Staffing services
- Waste recycling services
- Semiconductor production control software
- Stem cell therapy
- Supply chain management
- Business software
- Financial risk management services
- Diabetes drug discovery
- Pharmaceutical production

Every one of these bullets is attached, in my memory, to a particular, complex person. I usually visited members in their offices, but sometimes it would be over breakfast or lunch. We would pick up our conversation from the previous month and discuss new developments in their lives. There was an explicit understanding that these CEOs could raise any subject with me, whether it pertained to their business or personal lives, with the assurance that confidentiality would be absolute. They felt free to bring up issues that they might not be prepared to discuss with their boards of directors or their officers. In fact, these discussions frequently were rehearsals for potentially awkward discussions with business associates or family members. Many of the issues had to do with personnel matters, or pending deals, or transitions in their professional or personal lives. Though I could never deserve the trust that they placed in me, I made it my rule to be fully present to them and, in so far as it was possible, to listen with understanding. Rather than offering solutions to their unresolved issues, I hoped to help them to reflect on their lives and their work in ways that they might not otherwise be able to do. It goes without saying that there was an ethical aspect to virtually every one of their issues. You can perhaps see how it is that I increasingly understood my role as fitting with the Ignatian ideal of personal spiritual care, *cura personalis*. Over a period of nearly four years I conducted 830 such one-to-one meetings.

It is appropriate to ask whether a coherent picture would emerge if one were to inquire into the spiritual needs of business leaders. If the church is largely absent from their working life, what are the felt consequences? What is missing from their lives? A second question would be whether an enhanced religious consciousness would be good for business, and if so, in what sense, and how would it operate?

I was invited to join the staff of St. Timothy's Church in Mountain View, California to help develop a ministry directed at uncovering the spiritual needs of executives working in that amazing environment and then addressing those needs. This was to be done within the church, where permission to plumb the riches of the Judeo-Christian tradition was to be assumed. After six months of deliberation our design team settled on a small group format, which we named the Leadership Formation Group. Monthly meetings would take place in a conference room at the church, starting at 5 PM and ending at 9 PM. At 7 PM a supper of chilled water, freshly-made soup and warm bread with butter would be served. The evening would begin with *lectio divina* (reading of a religious text followed by silence), a brief presentation of a theological idea such as *grace* or *holiness*, followed by a free discussion of the theological idea, including always the question, "Would an awareness of this idea in a business leader be good for business?" The second half of the evening would be like a TEC executive session in that members would offer their unresolved business or personal issues to the group for their advice. Again, confidentiality would be absolute. The distinction from a secular TEC group meeting, however, was very significant. In this group we would enter into the discussion of secular matters out of a period of prayer, silence and theological reflection, and the discussion would include a spiritual dimension. The alpha group met for a year and a half at St. Timothy's. Much was learned. When the first meeting convened there was an air of excitement and expectation. Potential members had been told that their group would be led by a priest who was a physical scientist and businessman, and who had a number of CEOs in his care. As soon as they were seated I asked them, "What do you hope for?" Then I went to the easel and wrote rapidly as the words poured out of them. It quickly became clear that, though they wanted very much to engage the Christian tradition and learn more about it and to grow in business wisdom, their most strongly felt need was for integration of their lives. They wanted to find a way to end the compartmentalization of their lives. I understood this as a desire for personal authenticity. How could people of faith carry a secure sense of personal authenticity into their secular work environments? It was clear that this was not a matter of bringing a bible to work, or placing religious art in one's office, or proselytizing. It was about the interior life. This brief discussion took us immediately to the heart of the matter and provided the necessary focus for all that we did together. During this time I became more and more aware of the Ignatian character of my work. I began to read extensively about the life of Ignatius and the early Society of Jesus.

Around that time a Jesuit professor at Santa Clara University, who had heard from a student about my work at St Timothy's, asked me to develop a course for upper-division undergraduates. It would somehow connect practical business matters with wisdom from the Judeo-Christian tradition. It was to be taught as a religious studies course, but designed so that it could also be taken for credit as a business course. Undergraduates at the university, especially business majors, were very worried about what was going on in the business world just then. They would shortly be out there offering themselves, their personal gifts and their education in an environment that seemed very dangerous. The Enron and WorldCom scandals had recently unfolded. Could I help? "John, you would be credible to them." I agreed to do it, not knowing what it would entail.

I found no suitable course precedent. It took me a year and a half to write the syllabus. I did not actually know whether scripture and tradition offered much that could work in this context, nor whether what I found would be in any sense congruent with current business "best practices." This was not at all a straightforward matter for me. When I submitted the syllabus *Spirituality and Organizational Life* it was immediately accepted and placed on the academic schedule. I did not know whether anyone would sign up, or whether they would connect at all with the subject matter. As it turned out, a class of thirty-three signed up, twenty of whom were business majors, and ten of those finance majors. They were remarkably receptive to the subject, and a joy to teach. I found great consolation in this.

Ignatius wanted humankind to know, love and serve God, and to work out their salvation in their manner of living. He wanted to help them to do this intelligently by offering them spiritual formation, education and personal spiritual care. The very existence of the Society of Jesus constitutes a promise to the world, and every Jesuit institution is a bearer of that promise. This includes the Jesuit business schools, which have a particular role in developing leaders for the world's commerce. I had now been drawn into this work. I found myself actively collaborating at the heart of the Jesuit mission.

Decree 6 of the 35th General Congregation of the Society of Jesus, *Collaboration at the Heart of Mission*, concludes: "In his day, St Ignatius gave shelter to the homeless of Rome, cared for prostitutes, and established homes for orphans. He sought collaborators and with them established organizations and networks to continue these and many other forms of service. To respond today to the pressing needs of our complex and fragile world, many hands are surely needed. Collaboration in mission is the way we respond to this situation: it expresses our true identity as members of the Church, the complementarity of our diverse calls to holiness, our mutual responsibility for the mission of Christ, our desire to join people of good will in the service of the human family, and the coming of the Kingdom of God. It is a grace given to us in this moment, one consistent with our Jesuit way of proceeding."

As I read more about the life of St Ignatius and the early Jesuits, I was struck by their approach to service. What is distinctive about the Society of Jesus? Decree 2 of the 35th General Congregation of the Society of Jesus, on Jesuit identity, *A Fire that Kindles other Fires*, states: "It is in obedience, above all, that the Society of Jesus should be distinctive from other religious families. One need only recall the letter of Saint Ignatius, where he writes: 'We can tolerate other religious institutes outdoing us in fasting and in other austerities that they practice according to their Rule, but it is my desire, dear brothers, that those who serve the Lord our God in this Society be outstanding in the purity and perfection of their obedience, the renunciation of their will, and the abnegation of their judgment.' It is to the obedience of the *Suscipe* that St. Ignatius looked in order to highlight what it was that gave the Society its distinctive difference."

> *Take, Lord, and receive all my liberty,*
> *My memory, my understanding and my entire*
> *will,*

*All I have and possess; you have given me, I
now give it back to you,
O Lord; all is yours, dispose of it according to
your will;
Give me only your love and your grace; that is
enough for me.*

You can see how this shook my bones. Scratch me, and you will draw Jesuit blood. As this understanding unfolded, I came to understand that this was Cuthbert's response to my prayer. He had led me to St Ignatius.

***

My dear friend André Delbecq wanted to talk. He is a professor in Santa Clara University's Leavey School of Business and a former Dean there. He had been producing leaders for Silicon Valley's businesses and the wider world for decades, and something was on his mind. In recent years he had become focused on the interior lives of the leaders of organizations. He had daringly introduced a graduate seminar for MBA students titled The Spirituality of Organizational Leadership. This went beyond the emphasis on moral conduct that one would expect in a Jesuit university. It purposely engaged students in the contemplative work of engaging one's values and motives in conversation with the saints and mystics of several spiritual traditions. This had become a most popular course for MBA students. But after three years, they would be gone. They would be out there in the world, with all its challenges and temptations. How could he provide them continuing support? He did not want to just abandon them.

Now, this Monday September 4, 2000, fresh from a silent retreat with the Jesuits, he turned to me. Over dinner that evening he told me that he was sitting in the chapel at the retreat house in the presence of the Holy Family when the idea became clear. Would I join him in forming the Community of Joseph? The patron of this community would be Joseph the Worker, spouse to Mary and stepfather to Jesus. Our community would operate as in the monastic ideal, sitting in contemplation and prayer in support of leaders of organizations.

I was ready for this. I did not know what André would be proposing, but I was ready to say Yes, and we indeed went forward. For the three years that followed, until my move to Colorado, I faithfully spent Tuesday evenings in the rustic St. Francis Chapel at the Santa Clara Mission Church with the Community of Joseph. The evenings consisted of silence, *lectio divina* on three texts, silence again, free discussion on the texts and topics of concern to those present, intercessory prayer, and Eucharist. The door was open to André's present and former students and to Silicon Valley business leaders. This continues in my absence.

Ignatius was convinced by his associates to tell his story for the benefit of those who would follow him only after overcoming his concern over the temptation to "vainglory." He recounts the history of his life during the eighteen years following his serious injury in war. It is the story of a journey from ignorance to insight through the graces received by him in solitude, to the intense desire, which became a vocation, to share his insights with others. He became devoted to the spiritual well-being of his fellow man— to their education and spiritual care.

Holiness

I told my spiritual director that I did not want to be a saint. The conversation went like this.

We were about to begin my preparation for seminary. I wanted to establish a ground-rule for our discussions. I was ignorant, and that needed to be fixed. I needed to become familiar with the Bible and the Book of Common Prayer. I needed to know about the Christian tradition. I needed to catch up with the seminarians I would be joining. I wanted to be prepared. I wanted to be able to comfort people and to bring them hope. I would teach and preach. I wanted to be competent. But this was not about me. I was not motivated by vainglory, the thought of which was repugnant to me. It seemed that pursuing holiness could become a temptation. I did not want to go that way. As we were climbing the steps to the sacristy door at Trinity Cathedral, I told Canon Williams, "I don't want to be a saint." He stopped, turned toward me and asked, "What is the alternative?" I had no answer. So, we began the work of making me a saint. I trusted Canon Williams, and we just went forward.

I discovered that holiness and kindness go together. I found that I could classify people in two categories: those who spontaneously act as guardians of the dignity of everyone they meet, and those who do not. It is quite obvious, if you just pay attention. This understanding goes back thousands of years in the Hebrew culture. It was handed down to us by our Jewish ancestors. The word translated from Hebrew into English as *holy* is *qadosh, set apart*.

Closely allied with it is the word *chasid*, *(loving and) kind,* which also is translated as *holy*. Some examples from the Old Testament:

From *chasid*

> Psalm 86.2: Preserve my soul, for I am holy…
> Psalm 145.17: (is) righteous…and holy in all his works

From *qadosh* and its variants

> Leviticus 19.2: be holy: for I the LORD your God (am) holy
> Isaiah 6.3: said, Holy, holy, holy is the Lord of hosts
> Exodus 22.31: and ye shall be holy men unto me
> Numbers 16.7: whom the Lord doth choose, (shall be) holy
> Exodus 40.13: shall put upon Aaron the holy garments
> 1 Kings 8.4: all the holy vessels…in the tabernacle

We find in the New Testament the Greek word *hagios*, *set apart*, translated as *holy* as in these examples:

> Luke 1.40: For he that is mighty…holy (is) his name
> Romans 12.1: living sacrifice, holy, acceptable unto God
> Ephesians 3.5: now revealed unto his holy apostles
> 1 Peter 1.15: as he which hath called you is holy, so be ye holy
> Matthew 27.53: went into the holy city, and appeared unto

In these brief citations I see holiness in three kinds: the inherent holiness of God, who "fills the whole earth with his glory;" the holiness of dumb creatures like vessels, vestments, buildings or places set apart for God's good purposes; and the holiness of persons. In this last category we encounter confusion. It is here that the Prince of Lies can get traction. Our best weapon against him is truth. It is clarity of mind.

The essential mark of a holy person is obedience to God's will. By whatever life path an individual might take, this must necessarily involve continued discernment of God's will, that is, continued reflection on the vocational questions: What am I to do with the gift of my life? What is its best use just now, at this moment? How can I best employ my intellect and will? Should my life not be one of work and prayer? What is my appropriate place in society? The second mark of holiness in a person is kindness. It is the tender concern for those around us, whom we notice. We see them, and we care for their dignity.

This applies to everyone, but it applies especially to those in religious vocations, who are set apart in particular ways. We must regain our understanding of them as holy. I fondly remember the Carmelite sisters who taught us in Mount Carmel School in Socorro. We had infinite respect for them, in their cumbersome habits. And for our priest, in his cassock. We must shake off any awkwardness around the understanding of personal holiness. It is most desirable to be holy. Holiness is a choice, which we make every day. Let our vocations be shown in our clothing, our art and architecture, our music and our worship, for the greater glory of God and for the comfort of the people.

Scientific Truth

If our intellect is truly a gift from God, not earned or deserved but freely given, we have a responsibility. We must do our best to think clearly and to help others to do so, out of obedience to our Creator. If a philosopher is one who tries to help others to think clearly, then I must say that I am one of them. Out of whatever resources of education, life experience and reflection one can draw upon, a philosopher makes his offerings. In my case I resisted this role because I am not a fighter. I did not want to think of myself as a cracker-barrel sage, sitting in the general store and cracking wise. I would rather have stepped aside from such a responsibility. But I was restless. These ideas would not leave me alone. I kept coming upon fallacies imbedded in our Western culture that hurt people I care about. I want to arouse in you a passion for truth. In doing this, I want to comfort you and bring you hope. That is why I finally promised to write this book.

When I had newly arrived in seminary I expressed excitement that I could spend three years exploring the truth claims of Christianity. A woman seminarian in her second year of study replied, "You have your truth and I have mine." I was stunned. I did not know what to say. I learned later that this was a mark of postmodernism. I found that postmodernists cannot say clearly what they believe, but have a distinguishing characteristic in common: they are uncomfortable with the very *idea* of objective truth. In my seminary the usual response to the idea of objective truth was to attack the speaker as wanting to dominate others. This *argumentum ad hominem* is used with devastating effect: after all, a generous heart must allow for other points of view, not just what one person happens to think. I found that in the English-speaking West this way of thinking had infected our schools of liberal arts and our more liberal schools of theology, including my own seminary. In theology this fallacy is recognized as relativism. In all my years in aerospace, I had never met a postmodernist. I would not want to fly in a plane designed or flown by a postmodernist. An engineer must know the margins of safety of all the components of his aircraft design, and a pilot must never risk the lives of his passengers by exposing his aircraft to unknown dangers.

I am sorry to say that we scientists have contributed to the problem. It was with a heavy heart that I concluded that I must challenge fellow scientists. The problem is that some scientists have been careless with the truth and have joined the postmodernists. In addressing this problem, we must do our best to keep a healthy sense of humor, and we must try to be courteous. The core of the issue is that some of our most intelligent and hard-working scientists have become captivated by their own ideas and have drifted away from empiricism. This was surely the case with Einstein as he gave birth to his General Relativity theory in 1915. In 1905 he had burst forth on the physics scene with three landmark papers, including the one on Special Relativity. All were connected to physical reality by observations. Consider special relativity for a moment. In my radiation physics laboratories we used high-speed electronic instruments to routinely record events on the timescale of one nanosecond. The speed of light in vacuum is roughly one foot per nanosecond. The speed of an electrical signal on a coaxial cable is about eight inches per nanosecond. This was routine for us. It was also necessary for us to take into account the production of antimatter in our gamma-ray experiments, or we would get wrong answers. We were empiricists. We were quite comfortable with this. I was in the third generation to learn quantum mechanics, and I did not in any way resist its new ideas. I was certain of their basis in empirical reality.

With his theory of General Relativity Einstein had deliberately drifted off into pure thought. He performed thought experiments, rather than physical experiments. What he was doing at the time does not fit within my definition of physical science. It was not empirical. He was acting more like Plato. He was so pleased with the beauty of his ideas that, when asked what he would have done if some experiment failed to agree with his theory, he answered, "Then I would feel sorry for the good Lord. The theory is correct." Because of his exceedingly high reputation, others felt encouraged to follow in his footsteps. Our modern Physical Cosmology is the result. Its connection to physical reality is quite tenuous. It is the result of some of our best and brightest minds following in Einstein's footsteps. Modern physical cosmology combines Hubble's Law with General Relativity, to get what? I must remind you that Einstein never accepted the inherently probabilistic character of quantum mechanics. He could not accept it. He was sure that nature just could not operate like that. Quantum mechanics must be incomplete, else the phenomenon of entanglement would occur, in violation of his Theory of Special Relativity. We now know that quantum entanglement does, in fact, occur. It is a phenomenon of a different order from those phenomena constrained by the speed of light. Get used to it, Albert! As brilliant as he was, he was quite human, and fallible. Perhaps, if the recent observation of gravitational waves is confirmed, General

Relativity will become more an empirical physical science, and Einstein's physical intuition will be even more admired. But we must remember that this is in the end not about Einstein. It is about nature, and therefore, quite impersonal.

I feel it important to comment further on the fallacy of *argumentum ad hominem*. I must add that it works in two directions. It is usually employed to undercut the credibility of a speaker and distract attention from his arguments. It is intended to end any useful discussion of a subject. The same effect is commonly obtained by praise. If, for example, your teacher said that Thomas Aquinas had "a ten-thousand-pound brain," might your freedom to think critically about his ideas be compromised? Might you suffer a brain cramp whenever you had a diverging thought? As you read this book, do you feel free to criticize the ideas of Albert Einstein? Is he much too lofty an intellectual figure? Better not to even try, eh? Well, I want to give you your freedom. To place a scientist's work usefully in context, we can begin at either end: We can ask where his ideas came from, or we can examine the predictions of his theory and look for its successes. We can ask where the limits of physical science are to be found, and on what side of the line his theory falls. We can ask whether his theory had been imposed on us by the observation of nature by the instruments of physical science, as was the case with quantum mechanics. Let us begin with the discipline of earth science and then take a look at cosmology.

What do we actually know about what lies beneath our feet? How sound is "earth science?" What are we to think about those cutaway views of the earth's interior that appear in every earth science textbook?

In 1961, President John Kennedy announced that the United States would land a man on the moon by the end of the decade. He meant what he said, and he backed it up with action. The Cold War was on, and the Cuban Missile Crisis was about to happen. In sending men to the moon America would demonstrate its technical and economic prowess to the world in such a convincing way that the Soviet Union would be discouraged from challenging us. The Apollo Program unfolded on television with the whole world watching. Those of us who were alive in July 1969 can tell you exactly where we were on the day that Neil Armstrong first set a human foot on the surface of the moon.

In response to President Kennedy's announcement, the Soviet Union began a project to drill as far as possible toward the center of the earth. In 1962 the Interdepartmental Scientific Council for the Study of the Earth's Interior and Superdeep Drilling was created to conduct the work. It was a matter of pride to the Soviets that their own very good technical capabilities be demonstrated. This was as much the purpose of the work as the drilling itself. A site on the Kola Peninsula was chosen where it was thought that the earth's crust was rather thin. Drilling equipment with some very innovative features was assembled. Drilling began in 1970 and continued for a quarter of a century. Cores were brought up from deep within the earth, which were full of surprises. Alan Bellows, commenting on what was found, wrote: "Before the superdeep borehole project was undertaken, practitioners of Geology had reached a number of conclusions regarding the Earth's deep crust based on observations and seismic data. But as is often the case when humans venture into the unknown, Kola illustrated that **certainty from a distance is no certainty at all**, and a few scientific theories were left in ruin. One scientist was heard to comment, 'Every time we drill a hole we find the unexpected. That's exciting, but disturbing.'" (My emphasis added.) Here are the principal surprises from that project:

- Instead of the expected transition from granite to basalt at 3-6 kilometers below the surface, which was predicted based on seismic data, a metamorphic change in the granite was found, which was attributed to the high temperatures and pressure at those depths.

- More surprisingly, the rock was found to be saturated with salty water, which filled the cracks in the rock.

- Microscopic fossils were found in great numbers to depths as great as 6.7 kilometers. Twenty-four species of plankton were found, with carbon and nitrogen coverings rather than the typical limestone or silica. These remains were remarkably intact.

- The temperature rose with increasing depth much more rapidly than expected.

- The drilling mud that was brought to the surface fizzed with hydrogen gas.

The high temperature and pressure of the rock overburden caused the borehole to flow plastically and to seize the drill. The temperature by itself compromised the structure of the drill bit, and the scientists were forced to use refrigerated drilling mud to cool the drill in order to go just a little deeper. In the end they could go no deeper, and they stopped at the depth of 12.262 kilometers, or about seven and a half miles.

Now to the point: in so far as "earth science" and geology are physical sciences, I must insist that they be empirical, that is, that they be based on physical observations and measurements. The Kola project showed us that it is not possible *in principle* to go deeper than eight miles or so into the earth to make measurements or take specimens. It is about 4,000 miles to the center of the earth. Only eight miles out of 4,000 could possibly be explored by physical methods. That is two tenths of one percent of the way toward the center. The rest must be left to our imaginations. We must conclude that those cutaway renderings of the earth shown in every earth science textbook are works of the imagination.

So, let us speculate. Because we do not know the source of all the heat coming from deep within the earth, let us match the available data exactly. Let us make a hypothesis. Let us speculate that there is a fire-breathing dragon down there who breathes out just enough heat to produce the temperature gradients observed to the depth of eight miles, the region where our measurements are made. Because of the excellent agreement of the measurements with the hypothesis, this hypothesis could gain adherents, who might gather into a "dragon party," publishing papers and holding conferences. In opposition, a "non-dragon party" might form to oppose the arguments of the "dragon party." All might make a decent living from this.

But why is this not "science?" The answer is stunningly simple: This is not science because there could not be proposed *in principle* any way to disprove the fire-breathing dragon hypothesis. Proving a hypothesis wrong is decisive. It puts an end to the question. But there could never be an end to this question.

Therefore, according to the philosopher of science Karl Popper, this hypothesis must be permanently relegated to the category of "metaphysical speculation." This exposes a fallacy imbedded in our culture that does great harm. **It has the ugly name of "scientism." It consists in ascribing to science authority and competence that it simply does not, and cannot, have.** The spiritual harm it causes is mostly unintended, yet it is most serious. It makes us seem small and insignificant. We must be on our guard against humbugs.

We all know something of the story of the Wizard of Oz, but there are details that slip away from us with time. The original book was published in 1900, and the famous movie with Judy Garland came out in 1939. It recently occurred to me that some of the dialogue from that story could serve to illustrate some points I am making about the love of truth. We do recall that the Wizard was not a truthful man. On the contrary, he was a fake. I had forgotten that he was from Omaha, and that he was intensely homesick, until I got my hands on the book itself. It was full of surprises for me. I chose a lavishly illustrated publication offered by Sterling Press, which I heartily commend to you. Among my surprises was the fact that Dorothy's ruby slippers were actually made of silver. Of course, in any version, that story is a most wonderful adventure.

"We have come to claim our promises," said Dorothy.

"Has the Wicked Witch been destroyed?" asked the Voice, and Dorothy thought it trembled slightly.

"Yes," she answered, "I melted her with water."

"Dear me," said the Voice, "how sudden! Well, come to me tomorrow: I must have time to think." The Lion thought it might be as well to frighten the Wizard, so he gave a large, loud roar, which was so dreadful that Toto jumped away from him in alarm and tipped over the screen that stood in a corner. As it fell with a crash they looked that way, and they saw a little old man, with a bald head, who seemed to be as much surprised as they were. The Tin Woodman, raising his axe, rushed toward the little man, and cried out, "Who are you?" "I am Oz, the Great and Terrible," said the little man, in a trembling voice, "but don't strike me—please don't!" The friends looked at him in surprise and dismay.

"We thought Oz was a great Head," said Dorothy.

"No, you were wrong," said the little man meekly. "I have been making believe."

"Making believe!" cried Dorothy. "Are you not a great wizard?"

"Hush, my dear," he said. "Don't speak so loud, or you will be overheard—and I should be ruined. I'm supposed to be a Great Wizard."

"And aren't you?" she asked.

"Not a bit of it, my dear; I'm just a common man."

"You're more than that," said the Scarecrow, in a grieved tone, "you're a humbug."

"Exactly so!" declared the little man, rubbing his hands together as if it pleased him. "I am a humbug."

Is it possible that we are at times too polite? Do we ever ask a person in a position of apparent authority whether he knows what he is talking about? Of course, there are polite ways to ask one's doctor how he came to his diagnosis of some medical condition. We surely do not want him to fool us, and we do not feel it discourteous to seek a second, or even a third, opinion. Nor should the doctor be offended, because of our personal stake in knowing the truth. But do we dare to question an astrophysicist who tells us that we occupy only one of eleven parallel universes? Or a geneticist who argues that we are mere machines, fully explained by physics and chemistry? And that God is a figment of our imagination, created by us to give us a false sense of meaning and importance? Do we care enough about the truth to ask such persons whether they know what they are talking about and how they know it? Do we allow someone in a scientist's white laboratory coat to say anything he wants to about us and the universe that we occupy?

The next time someone pulls this kind of thing on you, try this: Ask him, "How do you know this?" If he gets angry, he will have exposed himself as a humbug, like the Wizard of Oz. On the other hand, if he is a true scientist, he will be glad for the challenge of explaining to you how he came to his conclusion: on what data he relied, and by what method of scientific inference he processed the data, so that you or his scientific peers could exercise your own judgment regarding the truth. A warning: when you hear the term "Standard Model," beware! This kind of language is used to suppress inquiry. It is coercive. There is no place for this in science. So, beware the Standard Model of sub-nuclear particles and the Standard Cosmological Model. If you run into someone who uses those terms, please do ask him whether he knows what he is talking about.

"You want proof? I'll give you proof!"

If striving for clear thinking is our loving response to our Creator, then loose thinking, permissive thinking, untruth, relativism, cannot be from God. If we acknowledge that there is an active spiritual contest for our minds, then surrendering to loose thinking could be understood as surrendering to the Prince of Lies. It cannot be condoned.

Let us consider the mountains on the moon. With his simple telescope Galileo thought he could see mountains on the moon. He could not quite be sure, but they looked like mountains. This caused some controversy in his time. As time went on, terrestrial telescopes of much greater power were built, and the mountains with their shadows could be seen quite clearly. Then we sent a lander to the moon, with a camera. The mountains could then be seen even more clearly. In July of 1969 man at last set foot on the moon. Bits of moon rock were brought back for examination in our terrestrial laboratories. This process can be understood as a process of increasing resolution of observations. There were surely mountains on the moon. No one could doubt it any longer. Then, what happened to Galileo's hypothesis? It was simply no longer needed. No one speaks of it any more. This demonstrates that **the purpose of a scientific hypothesis is to be made irrelevant by observation.** Let us now turn our eyes upward, toward the night sky with its many luminous objects.

How have our powers of observation of the cosmos improved since shepherds with their unaided eyes lay back on hillsides to gaze at the night sky? Very much, it would seem. The progression has gone like this: the naked eye; the astrolabe; optical telescopes of increasing size; particle detectors; telescopes observing in the infrared, ultraviolet, X-ray, gamma-ray and microwave portions of the spectrum; very large arrays. We see wonderful images from the Hubble space telescope almost daily in the news. The James Webb space telescope will soon be deployed. What richness! What progress! The resolution of our observations of the cosmos has very much increased, and we routinely make time-resolved measurements of spectra and their intensities. This is empirical. This is physical science, without a doubt—until we try to make sense of the data. We find that we have a problem: we do not have any *direct* way to measure the distances among luminous celestial objects. We must rely on a hypothesis.

This is where our love of truth is challenged. We must honestly confront the limitations of our instruments of observation. Although we now navigate accurately around the solar system, we cannot in principle place an instrument of observation very far outside it. We are, *in principle*, limited to making our observations of the cosmos from far away. Our most powerful telescopes cannot resolve any features of luminous celestial objects. We can only see a spot of light, though we can now measure its time-dependent spectral intensity. To us it must remain just a spot of light. **All of our raw data from observations of the cosmos could, with arbitrary accuracy, be displayed on a two-dimensional, spherical planetarium screen.** We cannot, by a strictly scientific means, obtain a depth dimension. The enterprise of physical cosmology depends entirely upon Hubble's Hypothesis, which is now called "Hubble's Law." This is the Big Fire-Breathing Dragon of physical cosmology. The "cosmological candles" are the Little Fire-Breathing Dragons, each with its own more or less complex hypothesis. **Because it is not, in principle, possible to make Hubble's Hypothesis irrelevant by observation, all of physical cosmology, which consists in making mathematical models of the universe, must be understood as metaphysical speculation.**

Here we stand on the earth, which by direct observation we can observe only to a depth of eight miles or so, looking up at the screen of a planetarium that shows all that we can observe of the cosmos. This is quite wonderful. Let us not forget that, of all God's creatures, we are the ones who were created to do the wondering. Metaphysical speculation is an honorable occupation. It is what sets us apart from the barnyard animals.

The stars have stories to tell. So it has always seemed to us humans. Perhaps that is why I wanted to be an astronomer — a namer of stars — when I was young. I followed many generations of our kind who turned their eyes and their thoughts upward toward the night sky, wondering at the vastness of space and our place in all of it. These days it is common to hear that we are actually made from stardust, encouraging us to acknowledge a kinship with the stars — a kinship in the flesh, most intimate. This is a new wrinkle on the ancient idea that the stars have things to tell us about ourselves. One might argue that the Enlightenment was about de-mystifying the cosmos. In the particular case of the philosophical discourse in France, there was a determined effort to do away with God and make do only with ideas that were secular and mundane — the more secular and mundane, the better. Though it might seem quite mysterious and wonderful, the idea that our bodies are made from stardust fits within that framework. Stardust is now to be thought of as secular and mundane, and, I suppose, so are we.

We do not possess many scientific facts about the cosmos at large. But we do have one dominant, objective scientific observation: whichever way we look out into space with a radio telescope, we see the same density of sources in the microwave portion of the spectrum. This observation is accurate to a few parts in a hundred thousand. In his 1993 book *Principles of Physical Cosmology*, Princeton Professor P.J.E. Peebles, the dean of American cosmology, wrote:

Modern cosmology is based on [a] simple characterization of the universe: that the universe looks much the same in any direction, and would appear to be much the same when viewed from any other position, as if there were no preferred center and no edges. [Either] we are at a very special place at the center of a spherically symmetric universe, or the observable universe is close to homogeneous. The former seems unlikely. The latter leads to the prediction of Hubble's law — that the apparent recession velocity of a galaxy is proportional to its distance — for that is the only expansion law allowed by homogeneity.

Here is the point: If the "unlikely" turned out to be true, then all of physical cosmology, as a profession, would consequently be false. We know that such use of the idea of probability is itself a falsehood: the uniform and isotropic distribution of celestial objects on a grand scale must be either true, or not. Since we could not find out by observation which is true, physical cosmologists must be content with their speculations about the structure of the universe. Peebles goes on to say,

> …our universe is quite close to isotropic, in striking agreement with what Einstein imagined. [However, our observations] do allow for a universe that is spherically symmetric, with a radial density gradient… But then we would have to be very close to the center of symmetry. This seems unreasonable, for there are many distant galaxies that would appear to be equally good homes for observers, with the one difference that in this picture

almost all would present observers with an anisotropic universe.

I must point out that this statement is not a scientific one. It simply reveals a bias.

On the hypothetical uniformity and isotropy of the cosmos on a grand scale: Is it true? From Roger Penrose's 2004 book *The Road to Reality: A Complete Guide to the Laws of the Universe*, beginning on page 717, we have the following words on cosmology:

> The discussion goes back to the Russian Aleksandr Friedman, who in 1922 first found the appropriate cosmological solutions of the Einstein equation, with a material source that can be used to approximate a completely uniform distribution of galaxies on a large scale... Basically, [such a model] is characterized by the fact that it is completely *spatially homogeneous and isotropic*. Roughly speaking, 'isotropic' means that the universe looks much the same in all directions... Also, 'spatially homogeneous' means that the universe looks the same at each point of space, at any one time... This pair of assumptions is in good accord with observations of the matter distribution on a very large scale, and with the nature of the microwave background. Spatial isotropy is found directly to be a very good approximation (from observations of very distant sources, and primarily from the 2.7 K [microwave background] radiation). Moreover, if the universe were *not* homogeneous, it could appear to be isotropic only from very particular places, so we would have to be in a very privileged location in order

for the universe to *appear* to us to be isotropic unless it were also homogeneous. Of course, the observational isotropy is not exact, since we see individual galaxies, clusters of galaxies, and superclusters of galaxies only in certain directions... But it appears to be the case that the deviations from particular spatial uniformity get proportionally smaller the farther away we look. The best information that we have for the most distant regions of the universe that are accessible comes from the 2.7 K [microwave] black-body background radiation [that tells] us that, although there are very slight temperature deviations, at the tiny level of a few parts in [one hundred thousand], isotropy is well supported.

From this we see that the isotropy and homogeneity that characterize the current cosmological models:

- Depend on Einstein's theory of gravitation
- Do not come primarily from direct observation of luminous celestial objects
- Depend heavily on the isotropy of the microwave background, as measured from Earth
- Implicitly depend on Hubble's Law

Cosmologists must rely on hypotheses. They entertain each other with their latest models of the cosmos, which seem often to change. And that is a scandal, because what physical cosmologists actually *do* is to write down those mathematical models of the cosmos. And they frequently change them because none of them works very well. For this reason they have us looking for "dark matter" and "dark energy" that are postulated to make up for gross deficiencies of their models, all of which depend on Hubble's Law. Cosmologists depend on this "law" because it seems attractive and compelling. They avoid the scientist's obligation to try as hard as possible to disprove his own hypotheses. Instead, sadly, cosmologists have ridiculed anyone who has suggested any other mechanism by which the frequency of light might change while traveling hundreds of millions of years through space. The possibility of discoveries of the second kind is not permitted. They insist that only the Doppler Effect (the Red Shift; Hubble's law) is permitted.

Karl Popper's classic book on the philosophy of science, *The Logic of Scientific Discovery* was first published in German in 1935. It was translated and published in English only in 1959. Popper was well educated in mathematics, and penetrated deeply into the subject of scientific discovery as it is actually done. Some quotes: "Whenever we propose a solution to a problem, we ought to try as hard as we can to overthrow our solution, rather than defend it. Few of us, unfortunately, practice this precept; but other people, fortunately, will supply the criticism for us if we fail to supply it ourselves. Yet criticism will be fruitful only if we state our problem as clearly as we can and put our solution in a sufficiently definite form—a form in which it can be critically discussed." To paraphrase his position: it could not matter less how one develops ideas about nature; the so-called scientific method is irrelevant. Popper was not a fan of induction. What matters is the statement itself: it takes the form of a statement about nature. Such an assertion, if carefully formulated, could then be fruitfully examined for the truth it might contain. But, how could we know in advance that such an inquiry would belong within science, and not outside of it, within metaphysics? The distinction between science and non-science is critically important if we do not wish to waste our time and effort, our gifts and education, on nonsense. Popper called this "the problem of demarcation." Considering the alternatives, he gave his answer: A statement about nature belongs within science only if it contains within itself the possibility of being disproven. He put it this way: "It must be possible for an empirical scientific system to be refuted by experience." Hence my example of the fire-breathing dragon as non-science. I have found Popper's thinking most helpful.

If the "big bang" and all the rest must be properly understood not as science but as works of the imagination, and if it is not so very difficult to find out, why did Prof. Peebles spend a whole career doing this? First of all, I must say that he would not agree that physical cosmology is merely metaphysical speculation. He would not use that language. He wrote in 1993 that physical cosmology was already "a mature physical science" and that he had "no reason to doubt" that Hubble's law would still be useful 10 years hence (that is, in 2003). So, why did he choose this subject for his career if it seemed so impermanent, so shaky, though arguably "mature?" His answer: "It never was my plan; in fact, my first reaction to cosmology was one of surprise that grown people could seriously care about such a schematic physical theory. I think I stuck with it because I enjoyed working in such uncrowded and fertile ground." But there must have been more to it. It was, after all, the stars that drew his gaze heavenward. And they do indeed have something to tell us about ourselves. They make it clear that we were born to gaze at them. We are the ones who were born to wonder. Nearly one hundred years ago, writing in the New York *Evening Sun*, Archy the Cockroach had this to say:

the men of science are talking
about the size and shape of the universe again
i thought i had settled that for them
years ago it is as big as you think it is
and it is spherical in shape
can you prove it isnt
it is round like a ball or an orange
providence made it that shape
so it would roll when he kicked it
and if you ask how I know this
the answer is that that is just what
i would do myself
if there are any other practical
scientific questions you would like to
have answered just write to
     archy the cockroach

The following text can be found on the inside flap of Don Marquis' book *The Best of Archy and Mehitabel*:

> [This book] showcases the hilarious free-verse poems by Don Marquis' irreverent cockroach poet, Archy, and his alley-cat pal, Mehitabel. Marquis' famous fictional insect appeared regularly in his newspaper columns from 1916 into the 1930s and has delighted generations of readers ever since; this selection is the first to be drawn from across his entire career.
>
> A free-verse poet in his former life, Archy has been reincarnated as a bug who expresses himself by diving headfirst onto Marquis' typewriter. Archy's sidekick

Mehitabel is a streetwise feline who claims to have been Cleopatra in a previous incarnation; together they give us a colorful view of life as seen from the underside. As E. B. White wrote in his now-classic introduction, the Archy poems 'contain cosmic reverberations along with high comedy' and have 'the jewel-like perfection of poetry.'

Darwin, the Human Genome and the Holy Spirit

One summer when I was seven years old our family spent a weekend in a log cabin in Wagon Wheel Gap, Colorado, near the headwaters of the Rio Grande. It was a tranquil moment in the life of our family. Richard and I had been put to bed and the door had been closed. I heard the comforting murmur of our parents' voices from the next room. Light filtered under the door, making the plaster ceiling look like textured parchment. I lay on my back, staring upward. How was it that I was seeing with these particular eyes? How was it that I occupied this particular body? Why was I in this particular place rather than somewhere else? Who am I, after all? The room began to spin, and I felt I was falling upward toward the ceiling. I have never forgotten that reverie, when I experienced the deep mystery of my being. It changed my life. I have ever since then been able to recollect that moment at will.

The question arises whether molecular genetics fully explains the human person. The scientific progression up to today goes like this:

- In his landmark book *On the Origin of Species* Charles Darwin brilliantly speculated that the evolution of species was a result of random variations, with the fittest surviving. He concluded that "Man with all his noble qualities…still bears in his bodily frame the indelible stamp of his lowly origin."

- The monk Gregor Mendel, with his experiments on garden peas, gave substance to Darwin's ideas by giving birth to the science of genetics.
- Crick and Watson, burning their brains to interpret a pattern of spots on a film, discerned the fingerprint of the double helix of the DNA molecule, giving birth to the science of molecular genetics.
- The Human Genome Project, led by Francis Collins, successfully completed its ambitious goal of completely mapping the human genome.

What does this tell us about ourselves? Why does the Christian faith of many top scientists remain unshaken? Are they not critical thinkers? Do they not accept the evidence of evolution?

We see almost daily in the press that we share more than ninety percent of our genes with the chimpanzee. Some well-known scientists argue that our self consciousness is itself just a product of evolution—that we are really just naked apes. Here are three example books taking that position: *The Naked Ape* by Desmond Morris; *The Selfish Gene* by Richard Dawkins; *The Astonishing Hypothesis* by Francis Crick. These authors are aggressive atheists, contemptuous toward those who disagree with them. They argue that we are simply material creatures, and that our sense of the uniqueness of our personal being is only a mirage, which will in time be exposed as imaginary. **This is called "philosophical materialism." Of all the fallacies at large in our Western culture, this one does the most harm to people that I know and care about.** It makes them feel small and of no account. I am moved to defend them. But how can I counter this assault on the significance of human life? How can I get traction against the popular culture? Our Venn diagram comes to the rescue.

We observe that the scientific progression recounted here has a direction: **Darwin's speculations have been made more secure as genetics has become more truly a *physical* science.** This is something to celebrate, and indeed, I do celebrate this triumph of human scientific inquiry. It has made genetics and the human genome in particular something that can be observed by the instruments of physical science—that can be *observed and measured.* In doing so, it has reduced the scope of speculations that can be properly called *scientific.* We know that it cannot explain our experience of identical twins, which are genetic clones. Our experience of human persons transcends the material. It transcends the power of language. It transcends the grasp of the human mind. **The human person remains a transcendent mystery that is experienced by everyone.** How good it is to acknowledge this, and to turn our eyes toward God, and our attention away from noisy atheists. Genetics, with its heritability of traits, is simply not the whole story.

We are empty vessels into which God pours his Holy Spirit—this God, who knew us in our mothers' wombs and breathed life into our nostrils. Our work on earth is to acknowledge this, and to turn toward God and those mysterious creatures, our fellow human beings. As much as we have in common with other kinds, as much as we acknowledge our kinship with them in the flesh, we are yet creatures of a different order, and not a "species" at all.

The Magisterium

I attended the 2006 General Convention of the Episcopal Church in Columbus, Ohio to observe whether the Episcopal Church would choose to discipline itself. The church was in crisis. In spite of formal objections from the Archbishop of Canterbury, the House of Bishops of the Episcopal Church had in 2003 approved the election of an actively homosexual man to serve as Bishop of Vermont. The Archbishop of York was to attend this General Convention to attempt to impose discipline from our Mother Church in England. Several resolutions were on the agenda pertaining to the Windsor Report, which addressed issues of authority within the Anglican Communion and asked the Episcopal Church to accept a voluntary moratorium on potentially divisive actions. The integrity of the entire Anglican Communion was at stake.

At this meeting the Episcopal Church gave the back of its hand to the Archbishops of Canterbury and York, the Windsor Report, the Anglican Communion, and good order in general. The Convention decisively rejected the voluntary discipline requested by the Windsor Report. The House of Bishops approved the election of a thrice-married priest to serve as Bishop of Northern California and they elected a woman to serve as Presiding Bishop and Primate. This had been a clean sweep for the so-called liberals. It was shocking to me. It was clear to me that, from the very early days of the Church, a bishop was to serve as not only the chief pastor of his diocese and an example of self restraint, but also as a guardian of the doctrine and discipline of the Church.

Doctrine and discipline could not be separated. Who could not see that by these actions the Episcopal Church was alienating Rome? No one seemed to care.

Not a word was said about the good work of the Anglican Roman Catholic International Commission, which had been working toward corporate reconciliation since 1967. Nothing was said at this Convention about their Agreed Statements on the Eucharist, Ministry, Authority, Salvation, Morals and Mary. The liberals blithely tossed overboard all the good will that had been cultivated with Rome since the Second Vatican Council. I was shocked that my priesthood had come to this. I was serving at the time as Rector of Saint Andrew's Church in Cripple Creek, Colorado. I simply could no longer explain to my parishioners and defend the official actions of the Episcopal Church. I resolved to retire at the end of the year and move to Washington, DC. I was a nuclear scientist. I would consult. I would make money. I would restore our finances. I would turn my back on my priesthood. I had been perfectly obedient, and it had come to this. It had all been a bad joke, and I had gone for it. I felt like an ass.

What can I tell you? The Church lovingly reeled me back in. The first time I attended St. James' Episcopal Parish in Lothian, Maryland the priest spotted me. I was wearing a necktie, but Fr. Bill Ticknor spotted me. When he came over I said, "I must confess to you that I am a priest." He said, "I know. I have been watching you." This good man had been the rector of the cardinal parish in southern Maryland for decades and had gently protected his people from all the strife in the church. He looked me up and began to call me "Canon Huntington." He asked me to preach and to celebrate the Eucharist. I was asked to lead the Adult Forum, which explored topics of the faith. I could no longer hide, nor did I want to. This was a large and most loving parish. Judy and I had found a spiritual home. Or, it had found us. We both sang in the choir.

But the dark clouds did not entirely vanish. At the risk of hurting people I care for, I must tell you that it was their enthusiasm for a particular book that tipped the balance. *The Shack* is a children's book about the Trinity. It is told as a story of a surreal encounter with God in three persons. It had sold eight million copies. People could not stop talking about it. I found it deeply offensive. I simply could not teach the Adult Forum from it. But my dear people insisted. In the end I agreed that, if someone else would lead discussions of *The Shack*, I would speak against it, offering orthodox teaching. We would see how that worked. It seemed to work for them, but not for me. It hurt me to be reminded weekly that the Church of England and its daughter churches in the Anglican Communion lacked a *magisterium*, that is, a teaching authority. These good people had not received authoritative teaching on the central Christian doctrine of the Trinity. But they were hungry to know, and they grasped at *The Shack*.

I have always felt that the separations that began with the 16th Century Protestant Reformation were meant to be temporary. I want to ask Protestants what they are protesting today. What is the Catholic Church doing that offends them *today*? What is so serious that this gaping wound in the Body of Christ must be left open to fester? Why is it good and reasonable to remain separated?

The Pope belongs not only to Catholics, but to everyone. Everyone is free to engage him in conversation. His writings and his speeches are available. The documents of the Second Vatican Council are available. They belong to everyone. We must ask what charity requires of us. Could we suppress the memories of past hurts and anathemas in order to freely and hopefully engage the Catholic Church as it exists today? Would the Catholic Church respond with generosity and courtesy? What is at stake? What current trends in Protestant ecclesiology and Catholic teaching act to impede the free exploration of paths toward reconciliation? Here we have powerful help. Although the Anglican churches are not permitted a *magisterium*, the Catholic Church offers its teaching to the world. It is summarized in the *Catechism of the Catholic Church*, offered to us as "what the Church professes, celebrates, lives and prays in her daily life." It was commissioned and promulgated by Pope John Paul II. It is intended to serve as a "valid and legitimate instrument for ecclesial communion." It costs ten dollars. If the Christian faith interests you at all, you should get a copy and argue with it.

During our time in Maryland the tug toward personal reconciliation with Rome slowly became irresistible. Judy and I had long discussions about this. We finally acted. We attended a Catholic "Anglican Use" mass in Baltimore, and Judy cried all the way through it. It was what she had longed for. Beautiful music, a whiff of incense, dignified language, and reverence for the Sacrament of the Eucharist. For me, the deepest draw was the knowledge that the *Magisterium* of the Catholic Church stood behind the liturgy and everything Catholic. The reception following the service was held in the undercroft of Mount Calvary Episcopal Church nearby.

That parish was engaged in an agonizing process of purchasing its freedom from the Episcopal Diocese of Maryland in order to join the Catholic Church. The room was filled with Anglo-Catholics, and a few Catholics as well. The air was charged with hope. Though I was wearing a necktie I was at once spotted by a senior Dominican priest named Carleton Jones. I told him that I was considering stepping off a cliff and becoming Catholic. He asked for a business card. I had none on my person, but Judy produced one. I know that, from that moment, that kind and wise priest has been praying for me. He became a close friend and my spiritual director in the months that followed. We decided at once to move to Mount Calvary and participate with them on their journey toward Rome.

Mount Calvary Church was founded in 1842 to bring the worship practices of the Oxford Movement to the Episcopal Church in the United States. The key figure in that movement was John Henry Newman, an English Anglican priest who ironically was to be received into the Catholic Church in 1845. We were to follow him 167 years later. For 170 years Mount Calvary served as a beacon of Anglo-Catholic worship in the Episcopal Church, and a thorn in the side of the Episcopal Diocese of Maryland. This was "high church," characterized by utmost respect for the Sacrament of the Eucharist. Mount Calvary possessed a tracker organ, ideally suited for baroque music. Our music director, Dr. Daniel Page, recruited singers from the nearby Peabody Institute to sing polyphonic music and Gregorian chant at the weekly solemn masses. The sermons were soberly and competently delivered, usually by the Rector, Fr. Jason Catania. I became one of four priests who served the parish. Fr. David Reamsnyder and Fr. Anthony Vidal completed our group of clergy. Together, we ushered the entire parish into the Catholic Church. Fr. Carleton Jones served as cat-echist and Chaplain, and when the time came, presented us all for reception into the Catholic Church. We formed deep friendships in this process. We were aware that we were doing something of historic significance. The leadership provided throughout this pro-cess by Fr. Catania was nothing short of heroic. The negotiation with the Episcopal Diocese of Maryland was grueling. We had to gain clear title to the church building and rectory and to other assets that could be freed, in order to present our properties unen-cumbered to the Catholic Church. This was finally accomplished. While doing this negotiation Fr. Catania offered support to several Anglican priests in the area who wanted to follow us by bringing their parishes into the Catholic Church. His energy never flagged.

On January 22, 2012 the big day came. The church was filled to the rafters. Friends and family had come from far away to share in the joy of the moment. Two orders of nuns in their habits were present, as were officials of the Archdiocese of Baltimore. Monsignor Jeffrey Steenson, appointed Apostolic Protonotary and Ordinary of the Personal Ordinariate of the Chair of St. Peter, had come to receive our parish and confirm us all. Ours was the first parish in North America to be received into full communion with Rome under Pope Benedict's apostolic constitution *Anglicanorum coetibus*. We Anglican priests removed our Roman collars. We were now, at last, Catholic. We were seminarians again. We were already taking a course of theological study from St. Mary's Seminary in Houston that was designed for former Anglican priests seeking Catholic ordination. You might be interested in the syllabus of the course of study from St. Mary's Seminary, which was focused on what might seem in some ways new and different to Anglican priests:

- The Petrine Ministry and Catholic Ecclesiology
- Catechesis and the Stewardship of the Catholic Tradition
- The Catholic Approach to Scripture
- Trinity and Christology: the Foundations of Ecclesial Life
- A History of the Catholic Church after the Western Schism
- Marian Theology
- Sacramental Theology
- Moral Theology
- Catholic Social Teaching
- A Practical Introduction to Canon Law
- Prayer and Spirituality
- A Practicum on Priestly Ministry
- A *Vade Mecum* of the Culture of the Catholic Church

In June Frs. Catania, Reamsnyder and Vidal were ordained to the Catholic priesthood by Archbishop Lori in Baltimore. My dossier had been sent to the Vatican months after theirs, and I received the *nulla osta* (a certificate stating that no canonical obstacle to ordination had been found) from the Vatican only in August, so I had to wait. But I expected to be ordained very soon. To expect to soon be a Catholic priest is to be filled with intimations of what is to come. I had been fingerprinted and subjected to a criminal background investigation. I had received a complete psychological evaluation. I had been trained on avoiding and identifying the sexual abuse of children. My application for ordination had been endorsed by the Chancellor of the Archdiocese of Baltimore. I was ready. But I would not ask when or where or whether I was to be ordained. In this most important matter I knew that I must be patient. I would be still and wait.

I visited the Vicar General of the Ordinariate at his office in Washington. It was time to talk about my assignment. I would, of course, go wherever the Ordinary might send me, but I had three suggestions to offer: I could stay in Baltimore to help build up Mount Calvary Parish; I could teach in a university as an Ordinariate priest; or I could go to Colorado to represent the Ordinariate to any Anglicans there who wanted to explore becoming Catholic. I knew Colorado well, having served as a priest for the Episcopal Diocese of Colorado, and we still owned a home there. The Vicar General said, "Go to Colorado. Write to Bishop Sheridan and tell him you are coming. Do this right away." I asked for and received his blessing. So it was that I wrote to Bishop Michael Sheridan of the Diocese of Colorado Springs, gave notice to our tenants in Monument, Colorado, and set in motion the moving of our household. I was to be a Catholic missionary priest in Colorado. I had my assignment.

I must tell you that all of us were eager to please Pope Benedict. We were so very grateful for his warm generosity in welcoming Anglicans into the Catholic Church. He was truly fond of our Anglican patrimony, including the rich use of the English language in the liturgy, the practice of Evensong, and of four-part Anglican Chant. The Book of Common Prayer was filled with most beautiful words, which we would not have to give up. We would have our own missal within the Roman Rite. It was almost too good to be true. As it turned out for me, it *was* too good to be true. After we had moved to Colorado, and after my first meeting with Bishop Sheridan, I received an e-mail from the Vicar General informing me that I could not be ordained after all because new guidance had been received from the Vatican to the effect that no more former Anglican priests would be approved for Catholic ordination for the Ordinariate who did not bring with them an existing Anglican congregation. I had done this in Baltimore, but I could not do it in Colorado. And that was that. I was on my own. I was dropped on Bishop Sheridan's doorstep like a dead fish. He had not asked for this.

Thank God, Judy and I were warmly received by Bishop Sheridan. I was not alone, after all. I began writing a monthly column on Faith and Culture for his diocesan newspaper, the *Colorado Catholic Herald.* I was asked to serve as Director of Adult Formation for St. Peter Parish in Monument, where we lived. I at last had the chance to teach the *Catechism of the Catholic Church.* This was not a small thing for me. It was published in English in 1994, the year that I had entered Episcopal seminary. I had kept it at my elbow throughout seminary and the years following. It had kept me on the rails during all of the conflicts in the Episcopal Church. It represented to me the love of truth that had always been present in the Catholic Church. Now, supported by a team of dedicated catechists, I could help former Protestants learn what Catholics know and live. I needed only to be sure that they were well informed and were completely free to choose, before presenting them for reception. Fr. Gregory Golyzniak, our Pastor at St. Peter Parish, trusted me with this work. He had concluded that I was Catholic enough. Fr. Lawrence Brennan, a seasoned seminary professor, taught some of the classes. We plainly shared a joy of teaching.

My religious vestments now hang in a closet: cassocks, albs, surplices, stoles, and clerical shirts. Sometimes I wistfully visit them. My Roman collars sit in a box in my dresser. You might on occasion see me in a cassock, but not wearing the collar. I am a Catholic man in Anglican Holy Orders, which I cannot exercise. I walked away from the Episcopal Church and my friend Robert O'Neill, the Bishop of the Episcopal Diocese of Colorado. I gave him up. This was not easy. I was careful to tell him why I was leaving him, but that did not make it any easier. Now I am home at last in the Catholic Church. God be praised.

We have retired to a patch of desert eleven miles outside the town of Deming, New Mexico. We call the place *Hacienda Far Niente*. Here I have found the peace to, at last, write this book for you.

The Lord bless you and keep you.
The Lord make his face to shine upon you and be gracious to you.
The Lord lift up his countenance upon you and give you peace.

John

The Feast of the Annunciation
2016

Afterword

How do I make sense of all this? Is my thinking settled? Am I at peace? Do I believe that the Universal Observer of quantum mechanics is God himself? Do the expectations and probabilities of physical science actually reside within the Mind of God? Do I really mean to offend the brilliant people who labor at the edges of physical science? Do I blame them for failing to distinguish science from metaphysics? Do I question their motives? What about those who explicitly embrace postmodernism? They are mostly students of liberal arts and Protestant theology, with a few scientists tossed in. Am I angry at them for hurting people that I care about?

I confess to feeling anger at a behavior that can be found across the intellectual spectrum: carelessness with the truth, without regard for the consequences. This behavior is most objectionable to me when I see people in positions of apparent authority misleading people just because they can, apparently for reasons of self-aggrandizement. I am sorry. This does make me angry.

Let us work our way through these questions, beginning with the two-slit experiment. Suppose we place the slits in randomly selected positions in such a way that we cannot see them. Put the mechanism with the slits behind a screen, and move the two slits separately in a random way using a robot, and then, at a randomly selected time, fix them in place. Guess at the positions of the slits, and write the guess down. Then look behind the screen. Do this several times to assure yourself of your ignorance of their positions. After this exercise is recorded in your laboratory notebook, proceed with the experiment. Once more, randomize the positions of the slits behind the screen, so that your ignorance of their positions is assured. Then turn on the particle beam as before. Let the apparatus run for a time sufficient to develop the image of an interference pattern. Shut down the particle beam and remove the screen. Record the positions of the slits and the pattern on the screen. Then compute the interference pattern that quantum mechanics *would have predicted* for those particular slit positions. You will find that the patterns match exactly. You will conclude that the probability density function, which is the interference pattern, could not have been expected by you, the experimenter, because of your documented ignorance of the slit positions. The expectation and probability that we are identifying here could not have resided in your own mind. But, because probabilities and expectations are states of mind, we might not stop here. We might be drawn across the boundary into metaphysics. We might ask ourselves, whose mind is this? Or we might resist the impulse. Maybe we should stop short of that question and leave well enough alone. We know what works, and perhaps that should be good enough.

The physicist Richard Feynman is a scientific hero to me. His advice on this was clear: stay away from metaphysics. Do not go there. He only wanted to know what works. He had the mentality of a safecracker. Either a safe opened, or it did not. He wanted to solve every problem himself. He knew that a scientist is a person who looks under the hood and figures out how things work. A scientist goes down into the grass, getting into the finest details of how things work. But he would not try to say *why* it works. Feynman said, "No one understands quantum mechanics." As much as he relied on intuition in coming up with new insights into physical reality, he was an empiricist *par excellence*, always referring to experimental data for guidance and testing of his ideas. He wanted always to be free to guess what might work.

But let us ignore this advice for a moment and "go there." Let us do a bit of metaphysical speculation. Let us consider some of the consequences of identifying the Universal Observer as God himself. That the expectations and probabilities of our experiment could dwell within the Mind of God would require that uncertainties must dwell there also. It would require new thinking on our part regarding determinism and free will. It would go like this. The experimenter creates specific uncertainties in setting up his experiment. Before he turns his apparatus on, just as soon as he has fixed the slits and the adjustable particle source, collimators and analyzers, the wave packets and the resulting interference pattern already exist in the mind of God, because at this moment we could do our quantum mechanical prediction of the outcome of the experiment. This is a particular kind of omniscience, which incorporates the associated uncertainties. When we consider the phenomenon of quantum entanglement, it would seem quite unsurprising to us that to observe the state of one particle would also instantly determine the state of a second, entangled particle, however far away it might be. This instantaneous coincidence is actually observed. It does not respect the limitations of special relativity, that is, the speed of light. To extend this beyond the laboratory, we could easily conclude that **all of reality dwells within God's oversight**. Here physics and metaphysics meet. The saints and mystics add their testimony. I find this speculation consoling.

The essential content of physical science is its raw data. Each datum carries with it an implicit pedigree describing the means by which it was observed and the accuracy of the method of observation. Over this increasingly large sea of data we lay our theories, laws and hypotheses in the attempt to make sense of it all. We look for simplicity (elegance), accuracy, generality, and predictive power in our theories and laws. That is what we scientists do. But not all scientists. Some feel free to cast off any tie to data in order to speculate more freely. Of course, no one could stop such very intelligent people as those working in string theory from doing this. I would not want to try. But I do object to calling it science. So did Feynman.

With regard to being respectful toward prominent scientists: we should try to be courteous, but we should also recognize it as a trap, especially for working scientists. Feynman said, "Science alone of all the subjects contains within itself the lesson of the danger of belief in the infallibility of the greatest teachers of the preceding generation." Consider the abuse of his authority by Lord Kelvin. It is a cautionary tale. He was confident that there could not be any source of heat within the earth; the temperatures in deep underground mines could only be the result of slow cooling from an early molten state. His recognized contributions to the subject of thermodynamics made him the most prominent scientist of his time. He argued forcefully that the earth could only be 100 million years old. He was sure of it. Because of his great authority geologists tried their best to conform to his estimate. But it did not work well. That the earth must be much older became accepted only later, after a discovery of the second kind: the radioactive decay of certain isotopes with the release of heat. There are other hypotheses for the generation of heat within the earth. But some-how heat is generated deep in the earth, contrary to Lord Kelvin's assumption.

The Standard Cosmological Model is based on two hypotheses:

- The cosmos is macroscopically uniform, with no center and no edges.
- The laws of physics are the same everywhere.

The first assumption is generally adopted by cosmologists because they do not like the alternative: that the solar system might be near the center of a macroscopically spherical arrangement of celestial objects. But the cosmologists have made their choice. The second assumption amounts to requiring that, should we be able to tour the entire cosmos with our scientific instruments, we would make no discoveries of the second kind. Such discoveries are not permitted in the Standard Cosmological Model. The application of Hubble's "Law" and Einstein's General Theory of Relativity has produced models of the cosmos that are internally inconsistent, leaving very large discrepancies that must be papered over with "dark matter" and "dark energy."

If the truth claims of physical science are scrupulously tested in this very objective manner, and if we give ourselves permission to be skeptical of them and the scientists who make them, how can we confidently engage the truth claims of the Christian faith? The same standards of objectivity clearly cannot be invoked. But if we are to enter the domain of meaning, value and purpose, which we must do, how can we proceed with confidence? I answer that we must become very still. Our physical bodies and psyches must serve as antennas for communication of the Divine Presence. We must be prepared for the null result. And we must be prepared for experiences that will overwhelm us. This is inherently unfair, because such experiences do not happen to everyone, and they can never be fully shared. Yet they are *experiences*. The Greek word for experience is *empeiria*. Christian faith is empirical. It is experiential. It is how the Church is refreshed in every generation. It is how faith operates. In quiet reflection we can take all the time we need to ask whether the saints, mystics and theologians down the centuries have seen and experienced the same thing. The effect of such grace as I have received is to remove any doubt.

I have found a spiritual home at the Benedictine monastery near Silver City here in New Mexico. I am very fond of the monks whom I have come to know. They sing Gregorian chant and use the Latin mass of 1962. They call me "Doc."

If I ever again say the mass, it will be from the beautiful new missal prepared for use by former Anglicans who have been received into the Catholic Church. It would be familiar to any Anglican, yet it is within the Roman Rite. I am comforted by this possibility, and I am at peace.

Appendix

Candidate Terms for Inclusion in your Glossary

- *Anglicanorum coetibus*
- antimatter
- apostolate
- Apostolic Succession
- Book of Common Prayer
- common sense
- *cura personalis*
- discoveries of the second kind
- dogmatic theology
- empiricism
- ecstasy
- fairness
- faith
- grace
- holiness
- human person
- interior life
- justice
- *kenosis*
- *Magisterium*
- megaton
- metaphysical terms
- mathematical physics
- obedience

- objectivity
- Order of the Holy Cross
- Oxford Movement
- philosophical materialism
- physical chemistry
- physical science
- postmodernism
- problem of demarcation
- quantum entanglement
- quantum mechanics
- raw data
- relativism
- sacrament
- Saint Cuthbert
- Saint Ignatius
- Saint John Henry Newman
- scientific hypothesis
- scientific law
- scientific truth
- scientism
- speed of light
- spiritual power
- theology
- theoretical chemistry

- valence
- virtue
- vocation
- worldview

***

Two Personal Examples

apostolate—A vocation, and therefore of the order of grace. Jesus said to his apostles, "You did not choose me but I chose you. And I appointed you to go and bear fruit, fruit that will last (John 15:16)." It is a life of radical obedience. This understanding fully answers the question that I asked of Saint Cuthbert. Writing this book was an act of obedience.

empiricism—A frame of mind that disposes one to value experience over speculation. This would apply equally to physical science and to theology. In examining our sensations or raw data, two questions are most useful: What is it? And how does it operate? Our description of a phenomenon must be accurate, and our interpretation of it must be sound. The difficulties are mostly with the interpretations, with the inherent temptation to speculate too broadly.

Bibliography

Abramowitz, Milton and Irene A. Stegun, Eds. *Handbook of Mathematical Functions with Formulas, Graphs and Mathematical Tables, First Edition.* Washington: National Bureau of Standards, 1964.

Aczel, Amir D. *Entanglement: The Unlikely Story of How Scientists, Mathematicians, and Philosophers Proved Einstein's Spookiest Theory.* New York: Penguin, 2003.

Anonymous. *The Catholic Sourcebook, Fourth Edition.* Huntington, Indiana: Our Sunday Visitor, Inc., 2008.

Baum, L. Frank. *The Wizard of Oz.* Illustrated by Charles Santore. New York: Sterling Publishing Co., 1991.

Bede. *Life of Cuthbert.* Found in the Penguin Classic *The Age of Bede*, Betty Radice, Ed. London: Penguin Books, 1983.

Benedict XVI, Pope: The *Apostolic Constitution Anglicanorum Coetibus with its Complementary Norms.* The Vatican, 2009. Available on the Ordinariate website at ordinariate.net

Berry, R. Stephen, Stuart A. Rice and John Ross. *Physical Chemistry.* New York: John Wiley & Sons, 1980.

Colman, Andrew M. *Oxford Dictionary of Psychology.* Oxford University Press, 2001.

Crick, Francis. *The Astonishing Hypothesis: The Scientific Search for the Soul.* New York: Touchstone, 1994.

Dawkins, Richard. *The Selfish Gene*. Oxford: Oxford University Press, 1989.

Diekmann, Godfrey. *The Laying on of Hands: The Basic Sacramental Rite*. Bronx: Proceedings of the Twenty-Ninth Annual Convention of The Catholic Theological Society v. 29, July 1974.

Dirac, Paul A. M. *The Principles of Quantum Mechanics, Fourth Edition*. Oxford: The Clarendon Press, 1958.

Dwight, Herbert Driscoll. *Tables of Integrals and Other Mathematical Data, Fourth Edition*. New York: Macmillan, 1961.

Einstein, A., B. Podolsky and N. Rosen. *Can Quantum-Mechanical Description of Physical Reality Be Considered Complete?* Physical Review **47** (10) 777-780, May 15, 1935.

Feynman, Richard P. (as told to Ralph Leighton). *"Surely You're Joking, Mr. Feynman!": Adventures of a Curious Character*. New York: W. W. Norton, 1985.

Frankfurt, Harry G. *On Bullshit*. Princeton University Press, 2005.

Franklin, R. William. *Anglican Orders: Essays on the Centenary of Apostolicae Curae 1896-1996*. Foreword by Hugh Montefiore. Harrisburg: Morehouse, 1996.

Gleik, James. *Genius: The Life and Science of Richard Feynman*. New York: Pantheon Books, 1992.

Harris, Sidney. Cartoons on Science: *"You Want Proof? I'll Give you Proof!"* There is no proof that the Foreword is by Albert Einstein. New York: Freeman, 1991.

Heschel, Abraham Joshua. *I Asked for Wonder: A Spiritual Anthology*. Edited by Samuel H. Dresner. New York: Crossroad, 1983.

Hughes, John Jay. *Absolutely Null and Utterly Void: An Account of the 1896 Papal Condemnation of Anglican Orders*. Washington: Corpus Books, 1968.

Hughes, John Jay. *No Ordinary Fool: A Testament to Grace*. Forward by George Weigel. Mustang, Oklahoma: Tate Publishing, 2008.

Lewis, C.S. *Mere Christianity*. San Francisco: HarperSanFrancisco, 1952.

Lindley, David. *The End of Physics: The Myth of a Unified Theory*. New York: Basic Books, 1993.

Lindley, David. *Degrees Kelvin: A Tale of Genius, Invention, and Tragedy*. Washington: Joseph Henry Press, 2004.

Marquis, Don. *The Best of Archy and Mehitabel*. Introduction by E. B. White. New York: Alfred A. Knopf, 2011.

Messiah, Albert. *Quantum Mechanics*. New York: John Wiley & Sons, 1961.

Morris, Desmond. *The Naked Ape: A Zoologist's Study of the Human Animal*. New York: Random House, 1967.

Pauling, Linus and E. Bright Wilson, Jr. *Introduction to Quantum Mechanics with Applications to Chemistry*. New York: McGraw-Hill, 1935.

Pauling, Linus. *The Application of the Quantum Mechanics to the Structure of the Hydrogen Molecule and the Hydrogen Molecule-Ion and to Related Problems.* Chemical Reviews, American Chemical Society, July 1, 1928.

Peebles, P. J. E. *Principles of Physical Cosmology.* Princeton: Princeton University Press, 1993.

Penrose, Roger. *The Road to Reality: A Complete Guide to the Laws of the Universe.* New York: Alfred A. Knopf, 2004.

Polkinghorne, John. *Quantum Physics and Theology: An Unexpected Kinship.* New Haven: Yale, 2007.

Popper, Karl. *The Logic of Scientific Discovery.* London: Routledge Classics, 1992.

Rahner, Karl, Cornelius Ernst, and Kevin Smyth, Eds. *Sacramentum Mundi: An Encyclopedia of Theology.* New York: Herder and Herder, 1968.

Rand, Ayn. *The Fountainhead.* New York: The Bobbs-Merrill Company, 1943.

Rand, Ayn. *Atlas Shrugged.* New York: Random House,1957.

Rand, Ayn. *The Virtue of Selfishness.* New York: New American Library, 1964.

Ratzinger, Joseph Cardinal, et al. *Catechism of the Catholic Church, Second Edition.* Washington: United States Catholic Conference, 1997.

Reber, Arthur and Emily Reber. *The Penguin Dictionary of Psychology*. London: Penguin, 1995.

Smith, Huston. *Beyond the Postmodern Mind: The Place of Meaning in a Global Civilization*. Wheaton, Illinois: Quest Books, 2003.

Smolin, Lee. *The Trouble with Physics: The Rise of String Theory, the Fall of a Science, and What Comes Next*. Boston: Houghton Mifflin, 2006.

Tarnas, Richard. *The Passion of the Western Mind: Understanding the Ideas That Have Shaped Our World View*. New York: Random House, 1991.

Tylenda, Joseph N. *A Pilgrim's Journey: The Autobiography of Ignatius of Loyola*. San Francisco: Ignatius Press, 1985.

Underhill, Evelyn. *Mysticism: The Nature and Development of Spiritual Consciousness*. Oxford: Oneworld, 1993 (first published in 1911).

von Campenhausen, Hans. *Ecclesiastical Authority and Spiritual Power in the Church of the First Three Centuries*. London: A&C Black, 1969.

Woit, Peter. *Not Even Wrong: The Failure of String Theory and the Search for Unity in Physical Law*. New York: Basic Books, 2006.

About the Author

John Huntington studied quantum mechanics at the University of Wisconsin, Brown University, and MIT before entering the defense industry. At the height of the Cold War he served as an interface between the physicists who designed nuclear weapons and understood their effects and the engineers who designed and built strategic nuclear missiles. His specialty was radiation physics. As the activities of the Cold War tapered off, he served the California aerospace community in developing advanced weapons systems and space transportation systems.

In middle age he experienced a call to the priesthood, which he could not deny. He was ordained an Episcopal priest and served parishes in California, Colorado and Maryland before converting to Roman Catholicism. He studied for the Catholic priesthood and was approved, but has not been re-ordained. He and his wife Judy have retired to a patch of desert eleven miles outside the town of Deming, New Mexico.